CLOSING IN ON GOD

*Faith, hope, love and laughter
in the second half of life*

Jim & Ann Cavera

MIDLIFE SPIRIT
Evansville, Indiana

*Dear Karen,
Best wishes
for growth in faith, hope,
love & daughter in Christ,
Love, Peace in Christ,
Ann & Jim*

1

CLOSING IN ON GOD:
Faith, hope, love and laughter
in the second half of life.

Jim and Ann Cavera at 1280 Cross Gate Dr., Evansville, IN 47710

ISBN 0-9710779-0-8

First Printing 2002
Mid-Life Spirit Publications
1280 Cross Gate Dr.
Evansville, IN 47710

Cover photograph by Harry Faulkner

TO OUR PARENTS
Joe and Lorry Cavera
H.T. and Gladys Smith
Your love, devotion and example have
taught us to savor the journey.

**TO OUR CHILDREN: JIM, KATIE,
CHRIS AND LAURA**
Your love and laughter have made
the journey worthwhile.

*With special thanks to
Rose Rogge for her gracious assistance
and Harry Faulkner
for the cover photograph.*

Contents

Introduction.... 8

CLOSING IN ON GOD

Faith, hope, love and laughter
in the second half of life

Thank you for allowing us to share the faith, hope, love and laughter we've found in the second half of our lives. We are grateful for your company.

Books have life only when they are read. After you've read our book, we invite you to sign your name inside the front cover and pass it along to a friend.

Peace in Christ,
Jim & Ann Cavera

Introduction

Are you old enough to be reading this? Welcome to **Closing In On God,** a book of reflections dedicated to faith, hope, love and laughter in the second half of life. We were once anxious to reach this stage in life when, at long last, we might have freedom to pursue some of the interests and dreams we postponed while the kids were growing up. Instead of dreading our empty nest, we looked forward to dusting off unfinished projects and studying travel brochures.

At least, that's what we thought waited for us. Now, on the far side of fifty, we find a whole batch of things we never expected. We have elderly parents who sometimes need more help than our teenage daughter. We also have adult children who still need our emotional (and sometimes financial) support. And don't forget the bills. We assumed everything would be paid for by now. Each month the bills still roll in as faithfully as the tide. In addition to our own problems, we often worry about friends. We've seen many of them terminated after many years of faithful employment, without even a note of thanks.

The one thing that does seem to work harder and get better with age is our faith, which we have honed through nights of our teenagers' trials and years of marriage. It seems the worse things get, the easier it is to pray. The more complicated life becomes, the simpler it is to trust. This in itself is both a comfort and a dilemma. We desperately want to pass on our hard-won faith to our children. They are either too busy or too far away to care.

We fear the most valuable treasure we have is being overlooked by the people we love the most, and that hurts. After struggling through life to gather a small store of wisdom, we finally have our priorities in order. When we look around, eager to share, we wonder if anyone is listening.

We have been asking ourselves why doesn't someone write about all of this? We've given it a try, sometimes writing together, sometimes separately. If you, too, find yourself in this exciting yet bewildering place in life, we invite you to join us. Together we'll explore possibilities for growth in faith, hope, love and laughter in the second half of our lives.

Jim and Ann Cavera

For everything there is a season,
and a time for every matter under heaven.
Ecclesiastes 3:1

Winter

Lord, in the winter of lives,
help us to renew our strength
for the coming spring.

Closing in on God
Jim & Ann

When we first began writing, we struggled to find a title to reflect the current circumstances in our lives. With our three married children now living in distant places, we are focusing all of our parenting skills on the one lucky teenage daughter we still have left at home. We have coped with frail, elderly parents who lived in a house down the street from us. Instead of buying formula and diapers for our babies, we bought Ensure and Depends for Grandma and Grandpa. God has a way of reminding us that we are not in charge. Time is a precious gift and we've learned not to toss it around lightly anymore.

Years ago a Christian professor spoke about how we start to die on the day we are born. We nodded our heads in agreement with his astute observation. Our minds acknowledged his point of view, but our hearts weren't the least bit troubled. We saw a vast ocean of time before us, and Death appeared to be asleep beyond a distant horizon. Only in the second half of life have we begun to comprehend how quickly the ocean of time is crossed and how seldom Death sleeps. We get an increasing number of phone calls from friends and family with news of illness and requests for prayer. One friend told us that he keeps a separate calendar for prayer requests to help bring names to mind so that he can turn them over to God.

As we begin closing in on God, useless attachments fall away and we grapple with the basic issues of life. We find ourselves making space only for the people or events we value the most. Short walks in the evening, visits with children and friends, home-cooked meals, good books, beautiful music and joyful liturgies are priorities on our list. The closer we get to God, the simpler our needs become.

To a younger generation, this sorting out, tossing away, slowing down process must appear as though we are losing ground. In reality, our feet are more firmly planted on the only ground that really matters. We are in a better position to hear our Father's voice through the call of the Spirit. We have crossed more than half an ocean of time, and most of us have had a chance to shake Death's hand at least once or twice. Beyond the horizon we see only a strong, sure, perfect light. It is quite a peaceful journey, to be closing in on God.

*****

How Can You Drive If I Can't See?
Ann

One frosty winter morning a few weeks ago, we set out to make a quick trip to the store. Jim grabbed the window scraper and cleaned off the driver's side of the windshield. As every wife knows, the rule is that both sides of the windshield have to be scraped. Off we headed, with him seeing clearly and me only half seeing through a glare of ice. I winced at every oncoming car as I squinted through my frosted windshield. Soon I turned to Jim and asked, "How can you drive if I can't see?" We laughed. After more than thirty years of marriage, there are many places in our lives where we both have to see in order to get where we're going.

Just as I like to know what is happening, even when Jim is driving, he likes to be helpful in the kitchen before company arrives. His gentle, guiding comments usually include, "Do we need this many vegetables? Are you sure this has finished cooking? We know this type of married behavior is common because not long ago in a restaurant we overheard a couple at a nearby table as they described a recent vacation. The husband said, "We went 1,500 miles in three days. She did all the driving. I just held on to the wheel." We knew what he meant.

We doubt such married behavior is new. Think of Mrs. Noah and the ark. Surely she must have stood by with helpful comments like, "Do you have to build it THAT big? Are you sure God said two of ALL of these animals? Did He really say FORTY days of rain?"

Marriage, too, is an ark. We build it beam by beam, sometimes smashing a thumb or two in the process. We make use of our unfinished, imperfect marriages to shelter ourselves and our children from life's worst storms. We walk side by side, yet remain independent. How many of us still recall the piece by Kahil Gibran about the pillars standing together yet apart? Somebody read these words from Gibran at every other wedding in the sixties. Weaving our lives together, independent yet dependent, we watch the road ahead while we ask gentle questions and lend our eyes and ears to each other. By now we are well aware of the holes in the road. Sometimes we drive around them while other times we plow right through. The truth is, neither of us can drive very well when the other can't see.

Hibernation
Jim & Ann

It is six a.m. The furnace is turned down low. A gust of icy wind rattles the bedroom window. Neither of us wants to be the first one to crawl out, slip down the hall and turn up the thermostat. We are quite comfortable, even toasty under our winter quilts. We procrastinate, trying to stretch out the peace and comfort of these last precious minutes between sleep and our daily lives.

In a sudden burst of inspiration we think: Why crawl out at all? Hibernation! That's the answer to these cold, grey days between Epiphany and Easter. Think of it. The frantic feasting of the holidays is over. We'll be like great grizzly bears and let all our extra pounds gradually melt away while we sleep. No effort required! The longer we ponder hibernation, the more sense it makes. No more driving through ice and snow for us. Not cooking or driving means we'll save big bucks on food and gas. Finally, think of the religious symbolism if we, as one, all arise from our beds refreshed and trim just in time for an Easter celebration.

While hibernation will remain nothing more than a winter morning fantasy, the human need to withdraw and replenish is real. This is not an easy time of year for many of us. In the last few years many articles have been written about Seasonal Affective Disorder or SAD. Attributed to a lack of sunlight, this is a mood disorder common during the winter months. One suggested remedy is to spend time in a sunnier climate during the short winter days up north. Another less costly remedy is to sit under special lamps designed to provide light rays to counter SAD. However, these can be pricey. One expert stated that common grow lights used for growing plants indoors will work just as well. Isn't it interesting that a light designed to grow plants might lighten our human moods?

CLOSING IN ON GOD

Bonus Birthdays
Jim & Ann

One January a few years ago, in spite of nasty weather and several inches of snow on the ground, our family gathered from far corners to celebrate Grandpa Smith's eightieth birthday. We pulled out all the stops in a bittersweet celebration. The cancer he had wrestled with a few years earlier had crept back with a stranglehold. The doctors shook their heads and said he had a few months or less. Some of the grandchildren made a banner out of a bed sheet and wrote in huge letters for all the world to see, "Happy 80th Birthday to the Big Cheese." We strung it across the front porch before dawn and left it up for a week. With a morphine pump hanging around his neck, he blew out the candles while we sang "Happy Birthday" so loud it must have echoed into eternity.

A few days later Grandpa gave away most of his important stuff to make sure it went where he wanted it to go. Then, with the good nature of one who is about to take a much anticipated journey, he sat down to wait. Hospice workers brought us a video that referred to "seasons" and "passages." Grandpa said he thought it must have been written by a professor somewhere. Always planning ahead, he told Grandma she would find him waiting for her just inside the Pearly Gates.

Spring went and so did the morphine pump. Now and then we sneaked Grandpa off for a few hours in his boat on his favorite lake. (Dying people aren't supposed to be out fishing). By the end of the year the hospice workers pulled out. Apparently Grandpa wasn't going anywhere anytime soon.

The next January, we crossed off the "80" on the birthday banner and added an "81." Not as many people stopped by this time. The morphine pump had been traded for little purple morphine pills. We weren't so careful about storing the banner

14

since we assumed it would not be needed again. After all, Grandpa's supposed departure date had been six months earlier.

The following year, we found ourselves frantically searching for Grandpa's birthday banner. We crossed off the "81" and added a few 82's. That day it rained really hard and the "Happy Birthday" and "Big Cheese" dissolved into puddles of red and blue marker. A few of us gathered and sang "Happy Birthday" two or three times. His memory wasn't so good any more. He kept asking if we had sung the birthday song. Every time he asked, we sang it again. The morphine kept him a little confused, but he still managed to beat his friend Harry in a few games of checkers.

All of this has taught us that life, no matter what shape it comes in, is precious stuff, full of unexpected twists and turns, even at the end. And doctors, no matter how wise, don't have the answer to life's final question. We decided that if another birthday rolled around, we'd let the grandchildren pick which bed sheet to sacrifice; and, next time, we would write with permanent markers.

*****

Downward Mobility
Ann

Everyone we know is trying to break bad habits. We've had our own faults for so long we have become quite comfortable with some of them. One habit that has been particularly hard to break is the desire to acquire more things. However, in recent years we have been trying to embrace Henri Nouwen's idea of "downward mobility." Basically, his idea is that, as Christians, having less allows us the freedom to do more and become more for Christ. We don't have to look far to find things we don't need. After more than thirty years of marriage and four children, we tell people that our home is like an archeological dig. The most recent layers are on top, and we have ancient artifacts buried in the bottom layers of the basement closets. For heaven's sake, how on earth are we to go about simplifying our lives?

We have been cleaning out closets and passing on mementoes to our children. As we rid ourselves of goods, we have also become aware of the clutter that stunts our spiritual growth. There are too many meetings to attend, too much fast food, as well as an endless variety of videos to watch when, too tired to think, we collapse in our recliners.

Downward mobility means letting go of our need to create more income, acquire more stuff, and be all things to all organizations. In the second half of life, we have found that our priorities have changed. Often, we enjoy nothing more than quiet conversation and peace at the end of the day.

At a recent meeting, Jim sat back and observed a young man who spoke with great passion about his plans to attain lofty goals. Jim recalled feeling this same passion to accomplish great things some twenty years ago. While he admired his young colleague's enthusiasm, Jim realized that he no longer shared the young man's ambitions. The need to achieve great dreams and amass a fortune along the way had been replaced with gratitude for all that we have and a deep appreciation for our ordinary daily opportunities.

It has taken us a long time to come to this place where we are ready to embrace the idea of letting go as a way of becoming more. We are finding that letting go of anything that no longer serves our priorities gives us a sense of fresh adventure and unlimited horizons. This new freedom is sometimes a little frightening, but we are finding that living with downward mobility leads to higher ground.

CLOSING IN ON GOD

John Lives!
Jim

The gospels describe the imposing figure of a man called John. No matter how we think of him, John certainly made his mark on the people of his day. Scripture scholars tell us that he was a "Nazir," one who had been dedicated to God from birth. Since a Nazir never cut his hair, John must have looked wild and scruffy by the time he came on the public scene. We are told that he dressed simply. Considering he lived in the wilderness on a diet of locusts and honey, he was likely on the thin side. Finally, we can say that John spoke his mind. Whether his opinions happened to be "politically sensitive" or not, he literally shouted his message over the noise of the crowds. If you met John, you remembered him.

Has there ever been a John in your life? Years ago, a young physician in training asked me, as the hospital social worker, to see an elderly patient and answer his questions about Medicare. That day I met briefly with the gentleman, answered his questions and moved on to several other cases. On the following Friday afternoon I received another order from the same physician about the same patient with the same concerns about Medicare. As this was the end of the week, I felt tired and more than a little put out by this second request. With my negative attitude, I rushed into the patient's room for a quick visit. At first I didn't see him in the darkened room. As I turned to leave, I spotted him sitting alone in the corner.

"I don't have much longer to live," he said softly. His words caught me off guard and left me speechless. For the next half hour or so he talked about his life and things that made a difference. All weekend I couldn't get him out of my mind. He had already gone home by the time I returned to work on Monday. A few weeks later I saw his obituary in the paper.

Today, we still make our way through personal deserts of loneliness, illness, and exhaustion. We regret things we've done or left undone. For me, that patient sitting alone in his room was John the Baptist. He didn't look especially odd and he never even raised his voice. Yet, he disturbed what had become my hurried way of life. John still lives in people who come into our lives unexpectedly and who, by their words and actions, bring us back on the road to the kingdom. Thank God, John still waits for us on the roads through our deserts.

*****

Finding the Dream
Ann

One benefit of having grown children in far flung places is that we sometimes get interesting letters. Last week our daughter Katie wrote to us about a visit she made to one of the four hundred small islands in the San Blas Territory off the coast of Panama. The Kuna Indians on these islands have maintained their traditional lifestyle in spite of the pressures of modern society. She described their religion as follows:

"They believe they are God's chosen people and that God wants them to live in peace and harmony. Any time anyone in the clan causes a disruption, the entire tribe is in jeopardy of not going to heaven. They don't have jails. They don't need them. They frequently have town meetings where people talk about any problems. It's just like a big group therapy session. Over the years several different missionaries have come to the island. However, since the missionaries fight among themselves, which the Indians know goes against God's plan, they prefer their own faith to ours."

In the first months of the year, we honor those who have struggled for our freedom, peace and unity. Beginning in January with Dr. Martin Luther King's dream of brotherhood, through Abraham Lincoln and his speech at Gettysburg, we dust off our most hallowed ideals and hold them up, hoping once more to make them a reality. We honor our heroes and renew our commitment to their visions. Even as we keep faith in our hope for peace, the reality slips away, always just beyond our grasp. Peace has become the Holy Grail of our modern civilization.

This is especially painful for us as Christians. In Christ's name we try to offer forgiveness and peace in our broken world. Yet, sometimes we can't even avoid arguing among ourselves. Would the "natives" of this world come closer to accepting what we have to offer if we did a better job of being peaceful and forgiving to other Christians? At times, lasting peace seems even further from our grasp than it did two thousand years ago in the time of our Lord Himself, or even than it did in the days of Abraham Lincoln or Dr. Martin Luther King.

Isn't it ironic that with all of our wealth, technology and sophistication, the peace we yearn for escapes us while it shines brightly among a little-known people on some obscure islands in a remote corner of a tropical sea?

*****

Praying to Win
Ann

In her book "The Season Starts Tomorrow," Katie McCabe tells the story of how Coach Walt Kennedy took the boys' basketball team at St. Jude High School in Montgomery, Alabama, from obscurity to the state finals. Though confined to a wheelchair by multiple sclerosis, Kennedy proved to be a much tougher coach than the boys had ever known. He disciplined them ruthlessly. While other teams played the less demanding zone defense, he insisted that his boys play their defense man-to-man. The boys learned to stand their ground and pound their opposition until it crumbled.

It occurs to me that we can pray the same way. As Christians, we use zone defense against evil when we pray together for world peace or an end to poverty. Group prayers offered for large evils are fine; but when it is our own child who is injured or a friend who has cancer, the struggle gets personal. I want to know that people of faith are lifting the name of my loved one to heaven's gate, dealing one-on-one with the hard thing that has come into our lives. When the adversary appears overwhelming, these are the prayers we count on to win our battles and nourish us in our pain.

I often think of my mother as one of the mightiest prayer warriors I've ever known. For more than twenty years she prayed daily that faith might sprout in my father's heart. Who can stand against such prayer? After twenty years, the wall around his heart crumbled.

One night I sat with Grandma at her kitchen table while she finished her evening cup of liquid supplement. She paused and said forlornly, "I feel so useless." Frail of body, dull of hearing, afflicted by dim eyesight and arthritic hands, she is unable to do most of the things she once enjoyed. "Are you still praying for us?" I asked, shouting a little so she could hear. She smiled broadly and nodded. "Then you are far from useless." She stood up and her gnome-like, ninety-pound body hunched over. If the prayer warrior within her were made visible, she would rise head and shoulders above mighty athletes. When times get really tough, instead of a team of less experienced zone prayers, I'll take one praying Grandma any day.

Gifts
Jim & Ann

We are still learning how to relate to our children now that they are adults and have lives of their own. When they were young, we often gave them advice. Somewhere between ages thirteen and eighteen, advice no longer worked and we discovered that they had become young adults. Lately, when our children come home, we admit that we feel a little awkward. Who are these people and what can we offer them? Our love remains overwhelming. From time to time, they reach out in small meaningful ways to let us know they, too, still remember the good times we once shared. As a way of forging a new relationship with our adult children, we'd like to offer them five free Valentine gifts.

Our first gift is unconditional love. The days when we focused on rules are over. We have become interested observers. Sometimes we wince inwardly at the decisions they make, or we hold our breath just as we did when they took their first steps. We still hurt with them if they stumble and cheer when they reach their goals. In spite of their choices and regardless of whether or not they call us, we love them. They live, not by our standards, but according to their own hopes and dreams.

Second, through our daily private dialogue with our Lord, we spread our prayers beneath them. Like an invisible net, prayer supports and nourishes them in a way that provides strength no matter where they are or what they are doing.

Our third gift is freedom. With prayer and love, we try to keep our mouths shut when it comes to criticism or advice. If they need either, they will ask. Not offering either allows them freedom from guilt which would only drive them away.

Fourth, we try to provide interesting role models. They are traveling the same roads we traveled. We are only a few steps ahead. We want them to glimpse aging as a rich, exciting opportunity to do more and become more. Always, we hope to be people they might want to become.

Our final gift is time on their terms as well as ours. We will understand if they need to be somewhere else or do other things, even when we wish it otherwise. We hope to be so joyful in their presence that we can continue to create good memories together. These are our Valentine gifts to them. Come to think of it, our Heavenly Father offers the same to us. This is not surprising since He is also a parent with children following in His steps.

"In my distress I called upon the Lord;
to my God I cried for help."
Psalm 18:6

Lent

With age we learn to lean on God
for strength in deep waters.

Grilled Cheese and Tomato Soup
Jim

I remember the season of Lent in my childhood as being the dark side of the year. The church waited for weeks in quiet, somber shadows and the adults in my life behaved much too seriously. Perhaps it had something to do with fasting. As children, we were exempt from fasting, but our teachers and parents still encouraged us to give up something. The trick was to avoid giving up anything too tough. If, in a guilty moment, we gave up something like dessert, well, we still had Sundays. Technically, Sundays were free days and didn't count as Lent. Sometimes we tried to give up things we hated, like cauliflower, but our parents and teachers were on to that ploy. As kids they had probably tried the same thing.

We kept our Lenten pledges on the honor system. One time, one of my classmates spread the news that he had spotted me eating forbidden Walnettos at the matinee. The chiding I received from the class hurt more than the frown from Sister Mary Louise. Lent was not my favorite season. In fact, I always seemed to get sick during Lent. Do you think it might have been from a lack of sugar? I wish I had thought of that reason back then.

Lent has changed a lot over the years. There are not as many rules. Fasting is down to a few days, and with a variety of frozen entrees abundantly displayed at the market, meatless Fridays are a lot more "user friendly." The young people of today don't realize how tough it was back then before the invention of pizza. All we had were limp grilled cheese sandwiches and tomato soup. Occasionally, a perch or two showed up on the table, but by the time you ate around the bones, you didn't get much.

It seems as though no matter how the rules change or what we eat, the real "meat" for Lent is always in the readings. Scripture takes us back to our beginnings with Abraham and our other faith ancestors and leads us to our end with the death and resurrection of our Lord. These scriptures provide a six-week course in Life. Here we find wandering and searching, sickness and healing, depression and joy, dying and rising.

As a child, I viewed Lent as a chore. At this stage in my life, the old rules of fasting and abstinence have taken on new meaning. A quick glance at my profile in the mirror is a strong argument that I might want to embrace a Lenten lifestyle on a year-round basis. What was once seen as a chore has become a "health initiative."

For many of us, this dark side of the year has become a welcome opportunity to look at ourselves both physically and spiritually. Lent offers a new opportunity to refocus our lives through our journey to Easter.

CLOSING IN ON GOD

Letters to God
Jim

A number of years ago, a college teacher had a group of students keep a journal. The rules were simple. They had to make daily notes in their journals, and they were not allowed to show these to anyone. He believed that people who put their personal feelings on paper experienced more satisfaction in their lives than those who did not. At the end of the semester, the teacher used some tests to compare the journal keepers with the non-writers. The results confirmed his belief.

Something about putting our thoughts down on paper frees us from the feeling of having no control over our lives. Perhaps this is why journals and letters were so much a part of our ancestors' lives. In today's world of instant communication with cell phones and e-mail, we still relish opening a letter and taking in all the words. For a moment, it seems we get a glimpse of the writer's soul. We recently found a postcard with a cryptic message that our older daughter once sent us from camp. She wrote, "Dearest Mom and Dad, We have one girl in our group who is really mean. I will tell you what we did to her underwear when I get home. Love, Katie." No child ever said so much in so few words.

Some notes can be prophetic. While this same daughter was still in high school, one day on a whim, Ann made a list. In no particular order she wrote down all the qualities she wanted in this daughter's future husband. Ann slipped the list into an old family Bible and forgot about it. Several years later Katie married a true soul mate who was not quite what we expected. Some time after the wedding we rediscovered the list. We could almost hear the good-natured laughter of our Lord. In large letters, the first quality on Ann's list was "Sense of Humor." Today Katie lives in

25

Hollywood with her truly terrific husband, who happens to be a comedian and a magician.

Writing can be as intimate an experience as praying. What better way to communicate with God during those times when we find ourselves unable to "say" a prayer? Some years ago during a particularly dark time in my life, I wrote a letter to God. He answered my written prayer. Our God is most patient. He enjoys hearing from us, even if it's been years since the last real contact. Why not jot down a note to Him? You don't even need a stamp. It is a relief to know that God takes our prayers seriously. He answers with wisdom, and perhaps now and then, even with a sense of humor.

*****

The Theology of a Leper
Jim & Ann

We came to know Freddie, the leper, in the mid-sixties' when we lived as Peace Corps volunteers in a small West African village. He had been one of the lucky ones who had received early treatment for his leprosy. He showed no ill effects from the disease. The lepers lived in a colony in an out of the way place north of our village. Freddie had a small house outside the colony gate where he worked at his trade. As did many of the patients at this colony, Freddie earned his living as a woodcarver. He often crammed a well-worn burlap sack with carved elephants, antelopes, fertility dolls and masks. With his bundle flung over his shoulder, he trekked the mile or so into town and peddled his wares. Peace Corps volunteers made easy marks.

Soon our small house displayed many examples of his handiwork for visitors to admire. We asked him to carve a horse, but he had never seen such a thing. So, we drew him a picture.

Unfortunately, the carving he produced matched the picture we had drawn. Next, we requested a crucifix. At first he seemed confused about what we meant. This time we found a picture for him. He remembered seeing a small one on the wall of a nearby mission.

Several months passed before we again heard his familiar greeting at our door. With anticipation, we welcomed him into our home. What Freddie pulled from his sack that day took away our breath. He had carved a crucifix about a foot high from a single piece of dark red mahogany. The smooth polished figure of our Lord hung with both dignity and sadness in stark agony. It brought to mind the long walk two thousand years ago between a certain government building in Jerusalem and the place outside the walls where common criminals met their death. Just as it did for us the first time we saw it, this crucifix still reminds us of the poor who are often crucified by hunger, poverty and disease.

One thing more still haunts us. The face of this Christ is African, but that did not surprise us. There is a familiarity about the face that brings back particular memories. The thin face, narrow jaw and high cheekbones still hold our attention. You see, Freddie had never been close enough to a crucifix to become familiar with the face of Christ. It seems he modeled the face of his crucifix after the one face he knew and understood the best. The face Freddie carved on our crucifix was his own.

*****

In the Potter's Hands
Ann

Some years ago I watched a blind potter work with a group of eighth graders. She gave each of the students a moist lump of clay and demonstrated how to make a pot with a lid. Each student began fashioning a pot according to his or her imagination. Some coiled thin ropes of clay around a base and upwards while others pinched the clay into bowls. Being eighth graders, they also caused pieces of the clay to end up as fake moustaches, earrings, or alien creatures which were not part of the potter's lesson plan. The kids presumed that the potter, being blind, wouldn't know the difference. However, the potter's ears served her well, and she was wise to the ways of eighth graders. She kept bringing them back to the task of creating a pot until they became absorbed in the assignment. The task proved more difficult than it appeared. Soon students were moaning when an almost finished pot collapsed at a critical point or curved in an unplanned bulge.

The potter followed the sound of each cry and gently took the broken pot in her hands. With agile fingers, she found the problem. Instead of smoothing the defect away, she deftly included it as an interesting feature in the overall design. The students were surprised and delighted each time the potter made something beautiful come out of an apparent disaster.

In a group discussion not long ago, some of us wondered whether or not God deliberately sets up trials and obstacles to test our faith. Frankly, I've always made enough mistakes all by myself to save God the trouble of manufacturing difficulties for me. When I realize what a mess I've made in my own life, then I am like the students of the blind potter who cried out for help. It isn't until I hand my "pot," mistake and all, over to the Master Potter that He can bring something good out of my tragedy.

God used the betrayal of Joseph by his brothers to save the Israelites from famine. He brought our salvation out of death on a cross. I can always trust the skill in the Potter's hands to salvage something both good and interesting out of the broken places in my life.

CLOSING IN ON GOD

The Waiting Room
Ann

Inside a certain hospital waiting room is a large fish tank. In this tank, water bubbles gently around waving plants while a dozen or so neon-colored fish drift in pristine water. Each morning an attendant drops exactly the same amount of food into the water. For a minute or so, a frantic flurry of activity follows the arrival of the food.

Pictures of flowers decorate the walls of this room while soothing music flows in from somewhere overhead. Dog-eared travel and hunting magazines are stuffed in a rack. Pamphlets in perfect condition, with titles such as "Going Toward the Light" and "The Other Side," remain untouched on a table.

Four times in two years I sat in this room with Dad while he waited to begin a round of radiation. The first time we came, Dad walked in, annoyed at the interruption in his life. The last time, he sat passively in a wheelchair as I wheeled him down the hall. That last morning, we heard friendly chatter coming from the room even before we entered. When we crossed the threshold, the people inside fell silent. The patients ahead of us were first timers. Living ahead of their disease, they were still hopeful. My father in his wheelchair was the specter of who they might become if they, too, had to return to this room for repeated rounds of radiation. After a minute or two, one middle-aged man resumed talking about his plans to go to Florida in the next few months. His voice rose, a little too loud, while he made sweeping gestures with his hands.

People disappeared into the room with the machine until only an elderly couple waited ahead of us. The man sat next to the fish tank, and he began taking roasted peanuts from his jacket pocket. One by one, he cracked the hulls and ate the contents. My father focused his eyes on this man's hands. Dad had little appetite and I doubted he wanted anything to eat. Instead, I wondered if he remembered, as I did, a certain apple-crisp autumn afternoon deep in the Appalachian Mountains ten year earlier. We had been sitting there together on a plank bench while we listened to Bluegrass music. That day, Dad had eaten roasted peanuts one by one until the hulls made a circle around his feet.

In heaven, beyond all the magnificent choirs of monks singing Gregorian chants, beyond all the banks of angels shouting Hosannas, there must be a grove of ancient pecan trees with plank benches and a wooden stage. And there, those of us who are so inclined can listen to fiddles, banjos and dulcimers while we eat peanuts until we are satisfied. Until that day comes, like the fish in the tank, we must keep swimming.

*****

Mareno
Jim

I served as an altar boy back in the 1950's. Since we lived near the church, my brothers and I were often called on for the extra services such as the Stations of the Cross and Benediction. This is where I first became aware of Mareno, a large Italian man with a thick accent. Although he appeared old to us, he spoke in a simple way. We understood that he had difficulty learning the more complicated things in life. He wore frayed clothing and stooped over as though he carried a huge burden when he walked. I remember being a little frightened of him at first until he quickly reassured me with his toothy grin and hearty laugh.

Mareno always made the extra services. He sat alone in the last pew and sang in a booming voice that out-distanced the organ at full pedal. Being a little off-key never stopped him from praising the Lord. My brothers and I did imitations of him, but not so that he or my parents heard us. We never got too close to him because a persistent odor of sweat and alcohol hovered about him like an invisible cloud.

The only direct problem Mareno caused in our young lives happened because we often drove past him on the street. Invariably, Mom slowed the car, rolled down the window and waved as though she had found a long-lost relative.

"Hi, Mareno. Want a ride?"

"No, Ma! Don't stop!" we begged.

She stopped. He squeezed in, thanking her profusely. Mom drove, all the while talking to him about the weather and asking about his health.

I don't recall seeing him around much as I grew into adulthood. Once, I spotted him at a local bar frequented by the college crowd. It seemed as though everybody knew Mareno. As usual, his voice boomed above the crowd and he appeared to be enjoying himself.

In March of 1975, I went back home to lay my mother to rest. For five years she had suffered with cancer. All through her illness, she had continued to think first of others. She knitted hats and mittens for her grandchildren. The favorite prayer she had embroidered and framed for us still hangs on our wall.

At the funeral home, the outpouring of sentiment from so many who had come to know Mom comforted us in our grief. Face after face filed past in a blur, some familiar, some strange, some young, others old and wrinkled. At the packed funeral liturgy the next day, the old Monsignor spoke about her as his friend. The Bishop impressed us with his appearance among the congregation. At the end of the liturgy, as we solemnly walked out behind the coffin, the Bishop waited at the door to speak to those who had come.

Then, something caught my eye. In the last pew, directly in front of where the Bishop stood, knelt an old man in a tattered suit. He sobbed in loud, uncontrollable gasps. Mareno. My heart gave way. I believe our Lord sent Mareno back into our lives that dreary Lenten day as a reminder that small acts of kindness often count for much. The real tribute to my mother wasn't that the Bishop came to her funeral. The real tribute to my mother was the presence of Mareno.

*****

Paradise Found
Ann

From time to time I see the elderly sitting alone with a faraway look in their eyes. It appears as though they have nothing to occupy their minds. Lately, however, I'm beginning to get a new perspective on the power of memory as we age.

While on vacation some years ago, we stopped at a nursing home in Florida to visit Aunt Lantie, who was then in her nineties. Our daughter, Katie, who was twelve at the time, had long, straight blond hair and she wore glasses, just as I once did at her age. As soon as Aunt Lantie saw us, her eyes flew wide open. "Ann! Ann!" she exclaimed, and she reached out to embrace Katie, believing that I had returned as the child she remembered. Memory suspended time in that moment.

Aunt Lantie had always lived with my Uncle Arvis, who was her brother. On Sunday afternoons in my childhood, my own brother and I sat on their back porch while we passed the time

32

listening to Uncle Arvis spin yarns about picking cotton in Mississippi before the turn of the century. Uncle Arvis had tomato plants growing right up to his back doorstep. He chewed tobacco while he talked, stopping now and then to single out a plant with one of his long bony fingers. "That one," he would say, and then he would nail his target with a long, true stream of tobacco juice. "Uncouth!" my mother yelled when she caught him. No video game ever provided a finer moment of entertainment.

For the first twenty years of my life, we lived by the sea. Not long ago a television story about crab fishing off the coast of Georgia brought back vivid memories from those years. I closed my eyes and walked once again along the shore at daybreak. The surf murmured at low tide. My bare feet stepped carefully around small beached jellyfish while I gathered only the most perfect flamingo colored shells. The morning breeze off the surf tasted of salt while a lone seagull screamed overhead and then plunged for breakfast.

What a wonderful gift it is to pick and choose memories the way we choose only the most perfect shells. The wise among us who step around the jellyfish in our past and horde exquisite shells have an eternal source of strength and joy.

On Good Friday, perfect obedience kept Christ on the Cross. I like to think that his memory of Paradise and infinite love sustained him in those darkest hours. While Mary wept with a broken heart, surely strength came to her from the memory of a baby smiling in warm, sweet hay. In memory, everyone is forever alive at the moment we choose to hold them. I no longer shake my head when someone I love slips away to a place I can't follow. Lately, it seems to be a particular blessing that as our bodies grow weaker, we have the strength of memories to take us to better times and places.

One who pricks the eye brings tears,
and the one who pricks the heart
makes clear its feelings.
Sirach 22:19

Spring

Lord, let us open our hearts
to hope in the spring

Leap of Faith
Ann

Spring begs for a leap of faith. That's what Peter made when he jumped out of his boat and into the water to meet the risen Christ. Once in a while, those illogical leaps in life can really pay off in unexpected ways.

We had so little furniture when the kids were babies that we kept our underwear on the shelves in the linen closet. Jim took an extra job to remedy the situation. So, imagine my bewilderment when he came home one night and announced that he wanted to spend all the extra money on a home organ. Small home organs called "Swingers" were a big thing that year. Music stores held public concerts in shopping malls. Crowds gathered to marvel at the stops and switches that made these mini-organs sound like a full-blown orchestra.

I really did not comprehend the madness that had overtaken my young husband's senses. He insisted that I go with him to a demonstration. As soon as I heard the magical music, I, too, became a believer. The chance of a lifetime opened before us. Our house would be a home where music lived. Never mind that Jim couldn't play any musical instrument and I didn't know one note from another. Soon we were flicking switches and pumping out symphony noises to swing with the best of them.

Before long, the novelty wore off. The organ gathered dust until our daughter Katie, at age four, discovered how many wonderful sounds this toy could make. We let her bang away. One day she surprised us by picking out songs we heard playing on the radio. From our first unreasonable leap of faith, other instruments followed, not only for her but for her younger brother and sister as well. In the last twenty-five years a piano, trombone, drums, guitars, banjos, dulcimer, flute, and once, for a few painful weeks, even an accordion have graced our household.

The underwear is no longer in the linen closet. Though, if we had to choose between a lifetime of music and a chest of drawers, you can guess where we'd still keep the underwear. The house is quieter now. Graduation and wedding pictures line the walls. Our pictures give mute testimony to the lively children who once made us so tired we fell into bed each night. We are quite comfortable surrounded by the mementos of our lives. With only one child left at home, we envision the day when the two of us will be alone. "What next?" we ask as we scan the shoreline for signs of Christ.

It seems there are two ways to age. Most of us look for Christ and when we recognize him, we stay in our boat and slowly make our way to shore, dragging our own particular nets of fish. Then, there are a few of us like Peter. Once we realize where Christ is waiting to meet us, we jump into the water, leaving our nets behind.

I don't think it matters much how we get to the place where Christ waits. After all, the net draggers provided the extra fish so that everyone could eat. Now and then, though, I long to be like Peter and leap unencumbered from the safety of my boat. If I ever gather that much courage, I think a husband with the wisdom to trade a chest of drawers for a houseful of music might be willing to jump with me.

*****

Acts of Nutrition
Jim

I have fond memories of making my first communion almost fifty years ago this May. Our class of about fifty gathered while family and friends packed the church on a clear, balmy Sunday morning. The girls delighted in showing off their white dresses and adjusting their veils. Most of us guys dreaded having to wear white short pants because they exposed our bony knees. To make matters worse, our moms had made us scrub those knees clean. We had to wear white shoes, too. Ugly and uncomfortable, these were nothing like the cool athletic shoes that kids wear today. Thank God we only had to wear them once. By the time my own sons made their First Communions, good sense had taken over and long pants with dark shoes had become the style.

On the Friday before that special day we all lined up for our First Confession. Each of us had been practicing diligently to memorize the confession prayers. I trembled going into the confessional for the first time. In the dim light I saw the outline of our pastor on the other side of the curtain, and I wondered if he recognized me. I remember the stuffy feeling of the small space and how I felt a bit overcome by the pastor's breath. Sister never warned us about that. Even though I forgot some of the prayers, the kindly pastor helped me through them. Years later, when my daughter was about to go for her first confession, I recalled these feelings when she tearfully revealed that she was afraid of forgetting her "Act of Nutrition." When you think about it, a seven-year-old's mistake can have deep theological truth. Taking the time to evaluate ourselves and share this with the priest in the Sacrament of Reconciliation is a kind of "Act of Nutrition" as well as contrition. Through the Sacraments we are nourished, not by traditional food, but rather by the grace of God. Many of the old devotions we practiced as children, such as a Novena or a May crowning, were meant to sustain us in faith on our life journey. As we celebrate our new life in the risen Christ, I cannot think of a better time of year for each of us to make an "Act of Nutrition."

*****

Trading Dollars for Dimes
Ann

In my mind I can still see our youngest son at age three, covering the table with fruits, vegetables and boxes of cereal as he helped me unload sacks of groceries. Standing on a chair, he surveyed the bounty. His face clouded over. "Where's the candy? Where's the cookies? There's nothing here to eat!" he grumbled.

I thought, *This is one of those teachable moments.* Taking out a dollar bill and handing it to him I said, "Next time I go to the store, you come with me. You can buy something you want with this dollar." I felt smug thinking he would soon find out how little a dollar bought.

Chris sat there for a minute, scowling at the dollar. Then, in a burst of fury, he crumpled it into a ball, ran to the trash can and stuffed it in.

"This thing's no good," he shouted. "It won't fit in the gum machine." How could I explain that the dollar he rejected was worth far more than the dime he thought he wanted?

Twenty years later, I am sitting with him at the same table in the same kitchen. He is eating a sandwich before he drives back to a distant university where he is a senior. Standing behind him, I kiss the top of his head, which I can reach only when his six foot frame is seated. I am trying to think of something wise and important to say before he goes back to his world of microwave pizzas at 3 a.m.

"Don't forget the Lord," I tell him. A pained look crosses his face and so I state the obvious. "You don't like for me to talk about this, do you?"

"It just sounds weird, Mom."

"Not weird! Before you were born, we dedicated you to God. This is who we are." One sunny day in the fifth winter of his life, this same child prayed for snow with such faith that he dressed himself in snow gear before he ran out to play.

Today I am frustrated and sad and so afraid that he will trade heaven's dollars for this earth's dimes that I forget how tuned in he always is to other people's needs. A few days ago, as though he read my mind, he brought me the very book I had been thinking about reading. This week he stopped at the Giant Peach farm stand and spent his meager resources on a jar of honey with honeycomb inside as a gift for his father. Am I so worried about religion that I overlook the goodness in his heart? Late that night I am still beating myself up. How could I be so heavy-handed? Why don't I talk less and listen more? Just before a new day begins, a quiet thought comes that makes everything right. So, my dear son, have you forgotten how to pray? Just wait till you have kids of your own.

*****

Springtime Adventures
Jim & Ann

One beautiful spring day we came home to find an odd assortment of twigs in the wooden arch above our front door. Thinking some trash had been blown there by the wind, we promptly brushed it down with a broom. Later that same afternoon, we found similar debris in the same spot. Robins had picked this unlikely place to build a nest. Of course, we realized they had made a foolish choice. They were trying to build a nest on a forty-five degree angle, directly above the traffic in and out of the house.

For a second time, we did the birds a favor and swept away the beginnings of their nest. Not more than thirty minutes later, an even larger collection of leaves and twigs appeared in the arch above the door. Who could deny such optimism? The nest stayed. The curve in the arch protected the baby birds from wind and rain. Neighborhood cats couldn't get near it. Seems the robins knew more about where to build a nest than we did.

Beneath the nest and beside the front door is the mailbox. This time of year stiff white envelopes with fancy script often turn up in the mail. Hold on. These are wedding invitations, but aren't they from children? Weren't we sitting on the sidelines at their ball games last month? Didn't we pick up a car full of these kids at the ice rink last week? We thought we heard them as teenagers watching videos and eating Cheetos in the basement last night. Now, they say they are getting MARRIED? We count up the years and are shocked to realize they are the same age we were when we got married. (True, but we were much older when we were twenty-three). Time has passed so swiftly that we wonder if we can get by wearing the same outfits to their weddings that we wore to their Confirmations.

Something about the force of new life in spring plants the hope of unlimited possibilities in our hearts. At least, that's the way the disciples behaved after the Resurrection. They had a great need not just to tell others about the risen Lord, but to travel to great lengths to spread the news. Setting out by boat or on foot, their hearts bursting with new life, they scattered faith like seeds on the wind.

This weekend our daughter will be rafting on a river in the mountains. Graduations and weddings will mark new beginnings for yesterday's children. Spring makes our youth believe anything is possible, and off they go on life's great adventures. Who can take a broom to such optimism?

*****

Mother's Day
Jim & Ann

Ever notice the things that mothers save? Tucked away in thousands of bureau drawers and musty closets are pencil holders made from juice cans, clothes pins fashioned into recipe holders, paper plates stuck together to form card holders, and hundreds of other crafts that have kept Elmer in the glue business for many years.

One of our all-time favorites was a carefully crafted and painted blue silhouette of a cat. It had a piece of sandpaper glued to it and the words "Scratch my back" written in a third grade scrawl. This prize hung over the Cavera stove to provide a way for

Mom Cavera to strike matches to light the burners. If this doesn't date us, nothing will.

Soon after our wedding, Mom Cavera sent a box of these precious mementos to us. Included were several "spiritual bouquets." Back in the 50's, some good Sister must have been delighted with herself for finding a way to tug at a mother's heartstrings while she made certain her little charges kept sending up prayers. Each construction paper card featured a carefully colored hand-drawn bouquet on the outside. Every flower bore the name of a prayer. No mother could resist a card that promised, "With all my love, five Hail Marys, four Our Fathers and two Novenas for you, Dear Mother." We doubt any such fragrant bundle ever saw the inside of a Catholic mom's garbage can. We weren't surprised when a box of this stuff made its way to our mailbox some twenty-five years ago. Since we can't bear to throw these things out either, they remain in a box in the bottom of one of our closets, presumably increasing in value each year.

A piece of bark decorated with acorns, straw flowers and maple seeds hangs in our kitchen. This creation once won the kindergarten prize in a school art fair. It has been hanging in the same corner since that day. Over the front door we have a pine cone wreath fashioned long ago by a foster son who still calls on special days. That's the way it is with children. They come and go, but not completely, for we keep visible pieces of their hearts.

Mothers know that the day will come when their children will leave for places of their own. A mother with mementos has proof that her children have hearts wise enough to fashion gifts of love. Years later, she boxes up these priceless treasures and sends them back to her children to remind them that no matter who they think they have become, their mother remembers who they really are.

CLOSING IN ON GOD

Grilled to Perfection
Jim & Ann

Jim begins: Small wisps of smoke rise from the neighborhood backyards. Whiffs of chicken, hamburgers and sometimes even steak waft on summer breezes. It's time to haul out the grill. One of the things I have inherited from my father is an appreciation for the preparation and consumption of grilled food. Over time, Dad owned a number of different charcoal grills. They all required a complicated lighting process which sent my brothers and me scurrying for sticks and newspapers. Half the fun was watching my father singe his eyebrows when he fired up the grill. With the invention of lighter fluid and the electric starter, the whole process lost its attraction. It's been more than forty years since Dad brought home his first Weber, a covered kettle type charcoal grill. For our family, the Weber produced meat, seafood and even vegetables that remain unsurpassed in my memory.

Ann joins the story: Shortly after Jim and I married, a delivery man arrived with our first Weber, a gift from his parents. One afternoon, we invited friends over for a smoked turkey, our particular grilled specialty. We put the turkey on in plenty of time, covered it and busied ourselves with other things. Shortly before the guests arrived, we peeked at the bird and were horrified to find it barely half done. I turned on the oven and handed Jim a pan from the counter. He brought the turkey in to finish cooking it indoors. In the emergency, I had handed Jim a pan that had been squirted with dishwashing liquid due to a prior use. Our guests arrived to find the turkey bubbling away in soap gravy. We ate something else that afternoon - crow, I think.

Jim and Ann: Fortunately for us, this type of gathering carries on hospitality in a Christian sense. Mistakes are easily forgiven. From Abraham, who served a picnic to the Lord under the oak tree at Mamre, to Jesus, who grilled fish on the shore of

42

Tiberias, simple food served outdoors has been a symbol of friendship. Food cooked outside tells our friends that we like them well enough to put ourselves out a little, but that we'd rather focus on them than on what we eat. Hospitality from our hearts and gratitude for those who come to share it fit in well with our faith. When one of our boys married, he asked if he could have his own Weber as a wedding gift. We were not surprised and more than a little pleased by his choice.

*****

Graduation Day
Jim & Ann

We sat beneath large trees on the lawn at Ball State University and watched our younger son graduate. That day marked the end of years of papers, tests, projects, late nights and long drives home. In fact, for the preceding twelve years, one or another of our three oldest children had been in college. So this day meant not only a day of great pride in our son, but also a day of unbounded relief for us as well.

We recalled this son's arrival twenty-three years earlier. At his Baptism, his older brother's first grade class danced in a circle around him. His four year old sister stood on tiptoe to say, "Thank you Jesus," into the microphone - words we echoed that graduation morning. Since his first graduation into God's family, there have been many other rites of passage as well: First Communion, Confirmation, driver's license, and high school graduation. As his parents, we fumbled along, sharing his adventures with games, lessons and friends. Above all, we have shared the joy of his love of music. As he packed his tools for survival in the world, we reminded him that whatever questions life asks of him, love is always the final answer.

A few years ago, a story circulated in our diocese about a monk at St. Meinrad Abbey who became ill and slipped into a coma. For a brief time, there was no visible sign of life. Then, the monk revived and began speaking about a near death experience where he felt himself moving through a tunnel toward a brilliant light. At the end of the tunnel, a voice from the light asked him one simple question four words long, "How did you love?" Can an entire lifetime be summed up by these four short words? First Corinthians 13:13 states clearly that only three things survive: faith, hope and love, and the greatest of these is love. As Christians, when we pass through our final graduation, the answer to the question "How did you love?" may well be the only one that matters. Not only have we been given the question for our final exam; we also have been given a lifetime to practice the answer.

*****

Memorial Day
Ann

Supposedly, an ancient curse said, "May you live in interesting times." This past century saw World Wars I and II, the Holocaust, and conflicts in many parts of the world, including the ongoing war between Serbs and Albanians as well as much senseless violence in our own country. This Memorial Day the bloodiest century in history is behind us, and most of humanity still doesn't get it. Each of us is someone's mother, father, sister, brother or child. We are each absolutely priceless and irreplaceable.

If we pause to take a breath and look around, we find our generation stands in a unique spot, historically speaking. It has been a thousand years since a generation stood with half a century of memory alive within them and a new millennium stretching ahead. We are the link between lives lost in the world's most terrible violence and a younger generation who will struggle to create a new age.

A thousand years ago, someone of sixty was ancient. The difference between our generation and theirs is that we have a second chance to use all that we've learned. Scratch the surface of any Second Halfer and underneath still breathes a 60's flower child, a 50's hot rod driver, or even a World War II veteran. We have become camouflaged by our middle-aged or older bodies. Who would guess that we are survivors of the most interesting of times?

We once had friends who either fought in Viet Nam or marched in protest against the war. Some believed love and peace would change the world while others dropped out and drifted into alternate cultures. Somewhere between singing "We Shall Overcome" and watching Neil Armstrong leave footprints on the moon, we cut our hair, packed away our tie-dye and disappeared into the jungles of parenthood. Inside, most of us still carry ideas and dreams begging to be heard. We ask: Now that the kids have flown the coop, is it safe to come out?

Christ fulfilled his mission in three short years. The message for us may be that it doesn't take much time for a truly focused, spirit-filled vessel to make a difference. With one foot firmly planted on either side of the millennium, our generation has an opportunity to speak out for change. Instead of sliding softly into the new age, what if we renewed our efforts and committed ourselves to fulfilling our dreams? The flower children of the 60's had some things right. War is dangerous to children and other living things. Love is the answer. In the opening years of the new millennium, we still have enough time to sing the true notes of a new song.

"The Lord will fulfill his purpose for me;
your steadfast love, O Lord, endures forever."
Psalm 138: 8

Summer

Summer comes with warmth and rain; still
the purpose of summer is not fulfilled
until the autumn harvest.

Father's Day
Jim

The invitation for the Cavera family reunion came in the mail last week. In early August, those of us who are able will gather in Grand Rapids at the house my father purchased for his family some fifty years ago. Dad has lived alone in this two-story, attic plus basement house since my mother's death more than twenty-five years ago.

Many parts of the house still reflect my mother's artistic flair. One bedroom ceiling, covered with maps from *National Geographic*, stimulates the imagination of overnight visitors just as it did for my brothers and me years ago. Guests are also surprised by a collage of old *Sports Illustrated* covers from the 60's that paper the basement bathroom wall. A vibrant Vince Lombardi and a young Joe Namath smile, there forever frozen in time. I look forward to visiting what has become a part of our family heritage.

The house has begun to show its age, but my brothers and I realize that it is also a symbol of our father and all that he means to us. We have always depended upon Dad to be there for us. Even when he disagreed with our choices, he never let us down.

Today, such stability is hard to come by. Dad taught us the meaning of faith by the way he lived. For as long as I can remember, he has attended Mass daily in the same church his parents helped found. We know he goes there to pray for his five sons, their families, and the families of their grown children. He seldom mentions this. For us, his constant prayers are a spring of pure water in our daily lives.

In addition to faith, Dad taught us the meaning of hospitality. He has often opened the house to provide a warm welcome for family and friends needing a place to land in times of transition. Grandchildren who were crossing uncertain bridges in their lives knew they could find a much-needed haven at their Grandpa's house.

In my grade school years, we spent summers at a small cottage on a lake. A huge oak tree by the back door stood out as the most prominent feature of this retreat. When two of us kids stretched arms around this oak, we barely touched our fingers. Some years ago, I decided to take my own kids to see the cottage. I didn't know how to find it because a subdivision of expensive homes now encircles the lake. My brother, Dave, told me to look for the oak tree, and he was right.

Today, it doesn't matter where we lived. While the house will always be a symbol to our family, Dad is the reality behind the symbol. His faith and hospitality are worth far more than any building. Families are blessed when they have fathers like oak trees for shelter.

Wedding Thoughts
Jim & Ann

On a beautiful June day our son Chris married his lovely bride, Angie. Together, we wrote the following words for our son and his new wife.

*****

To Chris and Angie on Their Wedding Day

On this special day, love is in the air and we hope to hang on to this feeling forever. However, that's not how life works. As unlikely as it seems now, there will come a time when you will look at each other and think, "Did I really marry THIS person?" Fortunately, this feeling, like all feelings, is subject to change. The point is that love based on feelings alone can be like riding a roller coaster that never stops. At first, it's exciting. Later, it just makes you feel a little ill.

On a second level, love is also based on commitment. It is commitment that brought you here today to state your vows in front of your family, friends, and God Himself. Unfortunately, even marriages based on commitment can sometimes be strained to the breaking point by hard times.

The third level where love is found is the level of faith. Having faith in the basic goodness of each other allows you to let go of personal expectations and embrace the life that comes to you. This love is like a gardener who looks at an empty plot of land and realizes that something good can be grown in the rich soil. He plows, plants, weeds and waters until the space he has is filled with abundance. Faith gives us the vision to see possibilities even when the ground is barren in the dead of winter. There is a verse in the Letter to the Hebrews that says: "Only faith can guarantee the blessings that we hope for or prove the existence of the realities that at present remain unseen." This kind of faith hangs on through inevitable uncertainties, misunderstandings, and hard times. It is the seed of hope that keeps us going even though we have no idea what the future holds.

Chris, not long ago you told us that a favorite childhood memory was of being with your siblings in the back of the station wagon where you read books, played games and ate snacks on the way to Florida. We were amazed that the journey itself meant more to you than the places we visited.

In marriage, it isn't the achievements or wealth that matter in the end. It's the shared journey that is memorable. To our son and his bride and to all who embark on marriage, we wish a love based on faith in each other, faith in God and faith in the loving, joyful future you will create together.

*****

Frozen Assets
Jim & Ann

We have two freezers in the house: one above the refrigerator in the kitchen, and a second one in the laundry room in the basement. As usual, both are full of good intentions. Once or twice a year we remove the contents and sort out our frozen assets. Today was such a day. Among the bounty we found two turkeys bought on sale at Christmas, cranberries left over from Thanksgiving, cherries we picked from the backyard tree last summer, and bags of exotic vegetables. "Exotic" in our house means a blend of anything other than peas, corn or beans. Also, we had a few containers with unidentifiable contents and a package of something labeled hopefully as "soup fixings." Originally, each of these things had a noble purpose.

2

As we sorted through the contents, we remembered all of the other good intentions we had left frozen over time. We still have many letters we intend to write, photo albums to make for the kids, a bird bath and flower beds we want to see in the backyard, exercise programs to start (again) and friends we want to visit. The problem is that the river of time runs faster than the stream of our intentions.

Every now and then we take inventory of our mental stockpile. Like the contents of our freezer, some ideas seem worthy of keeping while others need to be discarded. Even where faith is concerned, we still have plenty of good frozen intentions. At some point in life we plan to pray harder, study scripture more faithfully, devote more time to good works, and speak out more forcefully for peace and justice.

No matter how hard we try to catch up, we still find good intentions stored in every corner of our lives. Fortunately, it is easier to focus on the positive and take comfort in the intentions that we have turned into realities. As we get older, we worry less about food as well as intentions that must be discarded when we sort things out.

Tomorrow, a package of freezer-burned "soup fixings" will be in the garbage can by the curb, and we'll forget about flower beds for this summer. Meanwhile, we'll add "photo albums" to the shopping list for this week. Having a stockpile of frozen assets gives us plenty to choose from when we want to cook up something new in our lives.

Where's the Bus?
Jim & Ann

For many summers, we've sent our kids off to camp. They have been happy to go, and we have been happy to see them off. We sent them to scout camp, a couple of great Catholic camps and an endless string of band camps. We have been wondering if it will ever be our turn to spend a couple of weeks away at camp. We'd like to have someone cook our meals, take us on hikes and build our campfires at night. We ask for only a few small concessions in deference to our age and status. We need good mattresses for our aching backs, air conditioning and excellent plumbing in our cabin. Other than that, we're ready to rough it.

Come to think of it, since dreams are free, let's shoot the works on this one. We want broad, quiet trails through the woods with benches for contemplation (or catching our breath) along the way. Among the trees there should be a small stone chapel with fresh roses beside the altar. Let's add gardens with sheltered swings and bird feeders for taking in the beauty of God's creation.

Back at the camp, we'll have a personal trainer and chef to get us started on a fitness program. Entertainment at night will feature comedians with vocabularies that won't scorch our ears. We'll have a well-stocked library with a shady front porch and rocking chairs. (Notice how much of our fantasy takes place sitting down). In the craft barn, experts will show us how to make fishing lures or bake bread without a machine. Interesting speakers will give us ideas about what to do in our second childhood or sixty-five ways to amuse a grandchild on a rainy afternoon. We'll have discussion groups on everything from family reunions to home-based retirement businesses.

At lunch a while back, a friend confided she sometimes thinks about going off alone to a far away place. We've often felt the same way. The longing to be in a peaceful place where there is water for the soul and renewal for the body is universal. In the Twenty-third Psalm, David longed to lie down in green pastures and walk beside still waters. Like most of us, by the time David reached the second half of his life, he carried a lot of baggage. Perhaps, he, too, felt more than a little weary.

With God's help, most of us become rather proficient at coping. Still, sometimes we'd like to be wearing a name tag and waiting on a corner with a duffel bag full of old clothes to catch a bus and ride off for a couple of weeks at summer camp.

*****

Doctor Grandma
Ann

One Saturday morning, Grandma handed me her grocery list. At the top she had written: "Go to the pharmacy and get some bismuth powder." Pharmacist number one didn't know anything about bismuth powder. Pharmacist number two looked it up in his reference book. The only bismuth he found listed was as one of the many ingredients in a popular antacid. When I told Grandma that pharmacies no longer carried bismuth powder, she gave a heavy sigh of exasperation and said, "Mama used it for little scratches on all her babies." I realized she meant her own mother and the "babies" she referred to were her own nine younger brothers and sisters some seventy years ago. Seems it used to be an easy thing to get a little bismuth when you needed it.

Grandma often has me seek out one of her sure-fire home remedies: oil of citronella for mosquitoes, boric acid solution for a sore eye, Epsom salts for an infected cut. She uses these as her own personal duct tape for holding physical reality together. When things do fall apart, we head for the emergency room. This happens so often that Grandma refers to a certain physician there as her emergency room doctor. This is where we found ourselves a couple of weekends ago when, after puttering in the garden, she collapsed. After a bunch of tests, her favorite doctor sent her home with orders to rest and not spend two hours at a time outdoors in the heat.

After Grandma's cardiologist reviewed her tests, he summoned us to his office. "Your iron is dangerously low," he said. "Have you been taking the vitamins I gave you?"

Grandma told him that since she drinks a daily supplement plus soy milk, she had decided not to take his vitamins. She explained that she didn't want to be "over-vitamized." The cardiologist banged his forehead several times with the palm of his hand, leaned forward and asked gently, "Tell me, Mrs. Smith, just which medical school did you graduate from?"

She laughed and shot back, "Obviously, not a very good one." I decided not to mention the vinegar and honey concoction she drinks every night. He sent us away with orders to take the vitamins, plus some iron tablets.

It's a delicate balance we walk between home remedies and the marvels of modern medicine. I can only hope that some day thirty years from now, my own children will humor me by making futile searches for ginseng, garlic tablets and St. John's wort in a new millennium pharmacy. Every generation has its own brand of snake oil. The cold, hard truth is that bodies, like cars, eventually fall apart no matter how much we touch up the paint or what brand of oil we use.

Later, when I went back to the pharmacy to pick up prescription refills, idle thoughts crossed my brain. Grandma has a keen mind in a frail body that continues to function in spite of frequent dire medical predictions. I wondered what kind of shape Grandma's modern day medicine men will be in if they are fortunate enough to see their eighty-fifth year.

*****

A Wellspring of Faith
Jim

To enter the grounds of St. Meinrad Monastery deep in the hills of Southern Indiana is to enter a different world. Early one evening after a hectic day at the office, I drove out to St. Meinrad for a quiet retreat. It had recently rained. On the path from the outer parking lot to my room, I became acutely aware of the smell of lush greenery and the stillness. A few yards away, a solitary robin pecked at a tiny insect. I had almost forgotten the wonderful quiet of an evening in the country. Only one person met me on the path. She graciously changed direction to escort me to my room. That night I opened my windows to soak in the fresh air and quickly fell asleep.

Dreams of making this my permanent home were interrupted by a clamor of bells that announced to the countryside the beginning of a new day. I chuckled to myself as I remembered that St. Meinrad has a sunrise service every morning, not just on Easter. The monks gathered for morning prayer as the first rays of the summer sun peeked over the fields and lit up the very tops of the stained glass windows. St. Meinrad is on God's time. Morning is a time for praise.

The pace was slow compared to my average "work" day, but I never felt bored. God's time is full of the real business of life. We had much spiritual food to reflect upon and time to study and pray. With the absence of the distractions so common in the business world, I found myself more in tune with the rhythm of faith.

Ann has likened St. Meinrad to a wellspring where one finds fresh water, the kind that renews our strength and our spirit. Thirsty people have always sought out deep wells. Once, by a well, Jesus met a woman who was thirsty, more in spirit than body. The spiritual water she found at the well so delighted her she hurried to share it with others.

A wellspring is a special place where hope is renewed and Easter happens every day. We are blessed to have such deep springs close at hand. Sometimes, we forget that we are all connected to Christ, the true source of our living water. The retreat poured water into the dry channels of my spirit and helped me rediscover my own springs of faith.

*****

Love Into Being
Ann

Parenthood may be the most dangerous adventure any of us ever undertake. We know wonderful young adults who have come out of terrible homes. We also know devout, spirit-filled parents with children who cause them much pain. Everybody has ideas on how to bring up children. Sometimes it does seem to us that those without children often feel they are the greatest experts.

For instance, before our eldest child, Jim, came along, we knew exactly what kind of parents we intended to be. We planned to be potters and shape the "clay" we had been given into a wonderful adult.

Instead, we quickly realized that when it came to parenting, we were big time bumblers. No matter. Young Jim seemed interested only in how things worked. He wanted to know about science - only science. If it didn't involve science, it didn't matter. When he began to toddle, I learned to listen for the quiet. If things got too quiet, I ran to find out what he was up to. One day I went to another room while he rearranged the pots and pans in the kitchen. By the time I returned, he proudly displayed all of the canned goods, arranged by size with labels removed. We had surprise suppers for a month.

Who was this child and where did he come from? Instead of being potters, we were more like gardeners with a mystery plant and no instructions. We ran along behind him while he consumed one branch of science after another. We sat in the museum while he took classes on astronomy. His dad helped him launch model rockets while I prayed until they came home with their fingers intact. In junior high, he put a simple computer together from a kit. We took care of the burn when he absent-mindedly stuck his soldering iron instead of a pencil behind his ear. A favorite high school teacher spent one summer helping him get a ham radio license. When he got a chemistry set for Christmas, we held our breath through his experiments and tried to stay calm when he announced that something had "slightly caught fire." The word we most dreaded to hear coming from his room was "Oops." Today, at age thirty-two, he has degrees in Lasers and Physics and makes his way designing computer software.

Our oldest son did not get great parenting from us. We had absolutely no idea how to be parents. He did get all of our love and unending years of our prayers. In return, he taught us the truest thing about parenting; All children are mysterious, exciting, joyful gifts, meant to be nurtured, loved and treasured. When asked her secret, one elderly woman who had parented many successful, talented children replied that she "kept pouring love in until it spilled out of them." We'd like to add that even after our children are adults, we keep pouring in the love and praying that God will somehow correct all the mistakes we only now understand that we made.

When we were expecting our third child, young Jim's first grade teacher called to tell us about an exchange she had overheard between Jim and his classmate. His playmate had asked him if he knew how babies got born. Our son replied, "God loves them into being." Though not scientific, his answer was an absolute truth. God loves us all into being. Only occasionally are we fortunate enough to love our children into becoming the people God intended them to be.

*****

Driving Mr. Crazy
Jim

It's a summer evening and, except for a few walkers and a father teaching his daughter to ride a two-wheeler, the main parking area next to the stadium is empty. My mind is flooded with memories of running behind my children, holding on to the bicycle seat and shouting encouraging words. Gradually, they found just the right balance to propel themselves along the smooth blacktop. I remember the joy in their faces as they mastered a task they thought impossible. Tonight, I look at the young father with a twinge of envy. Those were the good old days.

I am riding in the passenger seat of our family car as my youngest practices her turns and gets the feel of the brake and accelerator. This is my fourth and final stint as the family driving instructor. By now, I should be comfortable in this role. This is not the case. Perhaps it has something to do with being past fifty. From where I am sitting, all the light poles and parked cars seem dangerously close. I know she completed the official driver's training course with a very good grade, but this is little comfort when we round the curve on a road that is much narrower than I remember.

I have always used intense concentration when learning a new task. Call me naïve, but I thought everyone learned new things this way. What I have discovered is that my driver-in-training has her own approach, which requires that certain type songs be playing on the car radio to enhance learning. In fact, one of the first skills she mastered was the ability to deftly switch between three stations without even looking. Finding the headlights and wipers took a little longer.

I have been making an effort to stay cool through this learning process, but I haven't been able to fool her. My sudden gasps for air and involuntary bracing motions have not gone unnoticed. Over the din of the music, she gives me words of comfort. "Relax, Dad." Perhaps it is the Lord speaking to me. Patience and trust are certainly His expertise. As parents, we never really stop worrying about our kids on the road. After the lessons, there isn't much we can do. Each time they slip into the driver's seat, we put them in the Lord's hands. We believe He doesn't mind the music.

*****

Laura's Turn
Laura Cavera

Ann's father, Grandpa Smith, passed away after many years of illness. We will always miss him, but he had a very full life and often expressed a wish to be with the Lord. At the time of his death, family obligations took up our time, and so we put our writing on hold for a week or two. During this time, our daughter,

CLOSING IN ON GOD

Laura, brought us a gift. The following essay is her reflection on what it is like to live with parents who are writers.

I am the youngest of four children and the only adopted child of Jim and Ann Cavera. There is quite a gap in age between my siblings and me. The next oldest is Chris and he is twenty-five while I am only seventeen. So, as you can see, I am pretty much the only one at home while Mom and Dad are writing.

I remember doing homework on school nights while my parents rushed madly around looking for their notes for an article. Sometimes they would be looking for the final draft itself. I saw the wild look in their eyes and the frantic look on their faces. It was better than TV.

Other times I have come home to find my parents having a brainstorming session. My mom never tells me or my dad what she is writing until she is finished because if she tells us, she forgets her great idea. I call it a predictable "senior moment."

One really annoying thing is that my parents see possibilities for writing in everything they do. They leave no stone unturned. We'll even be driving down the road on the way to church and I'll hear, "Hey! That would make a great article." I see my parents exchange a look and I begin to think, "Uh oh, here comes the next idea." As soon as we get home they write it down so they don't forget.

Sometimes Mom and Dad write something and give it to each other to proofread. Usually Mom says, "This is great. But...." And then the chaos starts all over again. Finally, when it has been proofread and written again and again, it is time to decide whose name goes at the bottom. A lot of times I hear, "But, Honey, he's your father," or one of my favorites, "You did most of the work."

I decided to write this because I've spent many nights watching the fun and the agony involved in being a writer. I thought it couldn't be that hard. I'm still deciding.

*****

The Last Adventure
Ann

After a long battle with cancer, Grandpa Smith left this world. Born in the middle of the first World War, he and his older brother lost their mother in the flu epidemic of 1918. Soon afterward, their father abandoned them and they shuffled, unwanted, from relative to relative until the Depression in 1929. No one needed two extra hungry mouths to feed, and so at ages thirteen and fifteen they hopped a freight train and never looked back. They shifted for themselves until World War II came along. The military provided the closest thing they ever had to a home, and so there they stayed. Many of those who made it back from the war got married and fathered the baby boom generation that is still driving our economy. My father's generation provided the heartbeat for the final century of this past millennium.

My mother, brother and I followed him from one military base to the next. We went from Jacksonville, Florida, to Charleston, South Carolina, where we sat on the sides of bridges and fished till our shoulders and legs were burned a deep copper. We climbed over rubble at Fort Sumter and heard stories of pirates and of treasures that he felt certain would surely still be buried in the sand beneath our feet. In New London, Connecticut, we played in snow for the first time while he welded together nuclear submarines. At Yorktown, Virginia, we waited until the tide ebbed, and then collected lead balls left over from colonial battles.

60

CLOSING IN ON GOD

You see, to H.T. Smith life was a grand adventure, and every day was a gift of unlimited possibilities. We went along for the ride. I was the "new kid" in school nine times in twelve years. From one base to the next, my brother and I bounced around on the back seat of the Chevy along with other things Mom gathered up at the last minute: a wash tub full of plants, the mop and broom and, once, a puppy.

We knew a few things for certain in our uncertain lives. We knew we were responsible for packing our own stuff, and for keeping up and that good people can be found everywhere. We understood that a home does not depend on the house you put it in. All were valuable lessons learned at an early age. Mother asked only one thing from life. She prayed daily that my father would become a man of faith. Her prayers finally persuaded him that faith is the only logical answer to questions asked by this illogical world.

In 1965 he retired to a cabin by a lake full of fish in Florida. Sometimes he looked up from his boat to catch a glimpse of a rocket launched from Cape Kennedy. That's where he was when men first walked on the moon. In between fishing, he made time to get his high school diploma and a degree from a community college. He lost his final battle to an enemy who, eventually, always wins. The sweet irony is that, in losing his final battle, this time he left us behind for the greatest adventure of all.

*****

Acre Peas and Spides
Jim & Ann

The week of Grandpa Smith's funeral, we drove more than 2,200 miles to be with both sides of our family. We left Evansville early on a Monday morning and arrived in Valdosta, Georgia, on

Tuesday afternoon to gather with family for Grandpa Smith's farewell. In all of our married life, we had taken our family to only one Georgia reunion fifteen years earlier. I wondered how awkward it might be to span the gap between my Southern aunts, uncles and cousins and our distant Indiana family. I shouldn't have worried. In Aunt Mary's yard, beneath oak trees heavy with Spanish moss, we hugged and were hugged by faces older, yet as familiar as yesterday. In the off-hand way Southerners have of offering overwhelming hospitality, Aunt Mary urged all of us to come inside and fill our plates.

Every flat surface in her kitchen had been covered with foods that made my dormant Southern taste buds spring to life. Aromas from smoked ham and turkey, okra and squash casseroles, assorted salads that neighbors had "dropped by," and several desserts mingled with a still-simmering five-gallon pot of Uncle Roger's acre peas. These small, oval, pale green peas are uncommon outside of southern Georgia. The farmers grow barely enough to satisfy local consumption. Uncle Roger had lovingly cooked those peas to perfection. We heaped praises upon him for his efforts. After supper Laura echoed our own thoughts when she said, "I can't eat another bite, but when will we ever get food like this again?"

The next day, after the funeral, we began the long drive back home. After spending Thursday night in our own beds and barely catching our breath, we left to be at our Michigan family reunion on Saturday. Here, too, we found ourselves surrounded by loving people, all labeled "family," and an abundance of food. The specialty of the day was an Italian shish kabob called spidie (pronounced *speedy*). These had marinated all night in special sauces before being grilled outdoors. Throughout the afternoon there were many references to the spidies and well-deserved praises for the grandsons who grilled them.

CLOSING IN ON GOD

On our way home at the end of this long, eventful week, our thoughts returned to the warmth and love that we shared with our families. Within each family there is an ongoing conversation that continues in spite of time or distance. The occasional coming together is like stopping by the side of the road for a common picnic in our separate journeys. Among us are rich and poor, educated and laborers. Nothing matters except that, because we are family, we are welcome. We remember the hugs as well as the warm conversation and real concern that make our families unique.

When Christ gathers his own at heaven's table, surely there will be love, laughter and food in abundance. All will be welcome. All will be family. We hope that somewhere in the abundance there will be a simmering pot of acre peas and a platter of spidies on the side.

CLOSING IN ON GOD

He said to them, "The harvest is plentiful,
but the laborers are few..."
Luke 10:2

Autumn

Lord, in the autumn of our lives,
help us bring in the harvest.

Time Shift
Jim

While at the Cavera family reunion in Michigan, my
daughter and I attended Mass in the church of my childhood. This
parish had been the center of my Catholic experiences from my
earliest boyhood to young adulthood. Although the building had
gone through extensive remodeling, I recognized many things. Yet
there were some startling differences, and these held my attention.
Where had all the people gone? Two-thirds of the pews remained
empty. I remember as a child being squeezed into pews by ushers
who never considered children as needing personal space for
praying.

That day, the celebrant appeared to be about the age of my
oldest son, a fact that has become common for me at this stage in
my life. However, his spirit of hospitality quickly made up for his
youthful appearance. My brothers and I had served Mass hundreds
of times in this same space. Now, we sat in the congregation while
we watched my eighty-two year old father serve in the role of
"altar boy." The readers and ministers of communion also
appeared to be about his age.

Somewhere along the line a shift had taken place. On that particular summer morning, I saw it for the first time. My mind filled with images of ill-fitting cassocks, incense, Latin prayers, sore knees, ever vigilant Sisters and gray-haired Monsignors who spoke in ominous tones. What happened here after I left home? At the end of Mass, I introduced myself and my daughter to the pastor and was comforted by his recognition of me as one of "Joe's boys." This said to me that my father's spiritual needs were known and being addressed, and for this I felt deep appreciation and gratitude.

There is no doubt that I am into the second half of my life. Through this experience and many others, I am reminded that I have shifted into a different dimension in time. The good news is that this is natural. In spite of being fatter, balder, slower and more emotional, I am coming to appreciate this place in my life. It is a time of new-found depths in relationships and growth in spirituality.

*****

Late Bloomers
Jim & Ann

One Mother's Day, Laura dug up a corner of the yard and made a bed for tomato plants. To encourage such a thoughtful gift, we bought three plants. The largest stood two feet tall and already had one medium sized green tomato. There is nothing like a little insurance for those of us without green thumbs. We bought a second, smaller plant with no tomatoes, but it did have several promising blossoms. Almost as an afterthought, we bought one sturdy, four-inch plant with no blossoms, just so we could honestly say we actually did grow one plant.

Soon, the green tomato on the largest plant turned red, and though it wasn't very tasty, we ate it. After producing this one measly tomato, that plant promptly withered. We don't know much about growing tomatoes, but we have seen children who, when forced to overproduce at an early age, often seem to dry up when they get older. Perhaps when children and tomatoes are forced to produce quickly, they have to draw on strength they need for roots and growth. The second plant with all the promising blossoms ran a mediocre course. By August a few tomatoes hung from it's skinny branches. Funny thing about that third plant, though. It grew slowly, putting down roots first, and then it outstripped the second plant. Now, in the early days of autumn, it produces abundantly.

Our neighbors have tomatoes in their yard: giant bushy plants with fruit billowing in clumps and clusters all over the place. They said the tomatoes they tried last year didn't do well at all, and so they had the soil analyzed. That's the trouble with both plants and children. Not only do they have to be watered and weeded; we also have to figure out what they are absorbing through their roots. At this point, our grown children are all producing at their own pace, and we are sometimes at a loss as to how to nourish them. Should we cultivate them a little more, try a different type of fertilizer, or simply stand by like a sturdy stake so that they can grab a little support now and then? Sometimes it's hard not to compare our tomatoes or our children with our neighbor's. Yet, the ones who put down the deepest roots may take the longest to bear the best fruit.

What about us? Now that we've produced a few ripe tomatoes, do we let ourselves wither? How do we find the energy to keep analyzing our soil, pulling the weeds and pouring on the water so that tomatoes, children, and even ourselves can produce the most abundant fruit in the autumn of our lives?

CLOSING IN ON GOD

Mercy or Justice?
Ann

One night last summer at the neighborhood Bigfoot gas station, a scruffy looking man in torn jeans waited beside a battered pickup truck. He had a pair of jumper cables in his hand. After Jim bought gas, this man approached him and quietly said that he and his family had just returned from vacation and he had no money left. Would Jim give him something for the cables so that he could buy gas for his truck? Jim had just spent his cash to pay our bill. He watched with relief as another customer traded the man a few dollars for his cables.

Was the other person foolish to give this man money? What if he was nothing more than a con man? Jim had no way to determine justice at the moment, and it really didn't matter. One of the most comfortable things about growing older is that we are becoming less concerned about charging a full measure for justice and more concerned with spending mercy.

Mercy is such a potent antidote that it takes a particular discernment to recognize the moment when it is the better choice. I like to think that the father and the older brother both loved the Prodigal Son. The older brother had a keen interest in justice. The father had the age and wisdom to understand that sometimes an ounce of mercy is worth more than a pound of justice. To appreciate the value of mercy, you must be old enough to feel remorse for foolish choices, able to remember ill chosen words, or know how it feels to be stuck without gas money a few times in your life.

One of the best things about mercy is that a few drops can often go a long way. In the "Random Acts of Kindness" movement, small gifts of mercy given at random to strangers become drops of oil that ease the burdens of daily life. The opportunity to smooth someone else's way is worth more than the small cost to us.

Sometimes justice is the answer that changes a life. Often it provides only a hollow temporary satisfaction for the victim. Like a pair of jumper cables, mercy coupled with wisdom provides a spark that can ignite a human heart when justice fails.

*****

Barbershop Blues
Jim

Last Saturday morning I went to the neighborhood barbershop for a haircut. It's one of those old-fashioned shops with traditional barber chairs, newspapers and sports magazines, and a row of uncomfortable waiting chairs along one wall. As usual, several men waited with their sons, each one clutching a worn-out plastic number. It reminded me of the shops I went to with my dad some forty years ago. Even the stories and jokes sounded familiar. It is comforting that some things remain about the same. The most notable differences were the color television tuned to a sports channel on cable and the women barbers who stood there working alongside the men.

Two things happened that morning to remind me of the passage of time. First, the barber implied that I didn't need a real haircut, only a trim. I have known for a long time that I have been losing my hair. In fact, I am well beyond the receding stage. Yet outside the rare occasion when I look in a mirror, I still think of myself as having a lot of hair. I acknowledged her remark with my usual good humor, and she got on with giving me a trim. When it came time to pay, I handed her my ten dollar bill, the cost of a regular cut in our Midwestern town. She asked me if I was retired, and I said with a bit of indignation, "Of course not!" She handed me a dollar in change.

As I went out the door, exchanging the traditional goodbyes, I glanced at the sign over the register. It read: "62 and over, $9." Reality hit me. Not only am I over the hill, according to my teenage daughter, but now a relative stranger had judged me to be even beyond my actual years. When I calmed down and shared this experience with my wife (we are the same age), she consoled me, and gently teased me at the same time.

What is it about aging that troubles us? As a Christian, shouldn't I be looking forward to the end of life and to being united with Christ in heaven? In my homilies I have often used the analogy of life as a journey. Recently, we traveled through the mountains of Virginia and took great pleasure in soaking up the grandeur of the scenery. It is with this same sense of wonder that we approach our experience of aging. Even though we anticipate the destination, we are still surprised by the swiftness of the journey.

*****

Cool Pants
Jim & Ann

In spite of our advancing years, we have been blessed with a teenager who frequently brings us up to date on what is happening in the real world. She recently shared her theory with us about the direct relationship between the height of a person's pants and his age. She is convinced that the older the person, the higher the pants. What she is referring to is the location of the waistband. She may be on to something. No matter where we go, we see young people wearing pants with so much sag, we're not sure what's holding them up. In fact, the recent trend seems to be the baggier the better. That's the "cool" look, or so we have been told. From our observations, we have concluded that baggy pants are indeed cool as they have a lot of space inside for air to circulate. There must have been a shortage of material back in the 50's as our pants had a snug fit and the legs rode up to reveal most of our white socks. That's how we knew we looked "cool."

Not long ago a college student drove by in a sporty red convertible. He had the self-confident look of a young man in a "cool" car. We obliged him by turning our heads to admire the view, and then a strange thing happened. Our thoughts turned to wondering how he could afford the payments and who was footing the insurance bill. Lately, we often find ourselves doing this kind of thing. When we see a luxury vehicle or estate, we speculate a little about payments, taxes, insurance and the cost of upkeep. Time has changed our priorities. We are no longer worried as much about looking "cool" as we are about feeling "cool" inside. For example, it feels "cool" to us not to pay more for things than we can afford.

When we bought our last car, our first priority was how it felt. Did it ride well? Did it have a well-padded seat? We chose carefully, then drove our new "previously owned" vehicle into the driveway. Our teenager's first reaction was that we had bought an "old people's" car. Come to think of it, we don't believe that we have ever seen a teenager driving a white, four-door sedan with vinyl trim.

Second Halfers have a different focus, not only about clothes and cars, but about life. Looks count for little. "Cool" is being comfortable, not only with what we have, but with who we are. As we see past the surface, we move ever closer to inner harmony in mind, body and soul. For us, that's not only real - that's "cool."

70

CLOSING IN ON GOD

Going Under or Staying Afloat?
Ann

Some time ago, I followed my mother through the crowded aisles of a nearby "dollar" store. She piled dusty candy bars, cookies at two bags for a dollar, yet another throw pillow, a new lampshade, four plastic place mats and assorted knickknacks into her cart. I kept telling myself that God's plan for me was to have infinite patience with Mom, that I really had nothing more important on earth to do than to be there with her. Aisle after aisle we crept. I pushed the cart slowly, an inch at the time while she considered the merits of one household item over another.

At one point she leaned close to my ear and whispered, "See how much you could save by shopping here?"

I am in agony. I want to scream. Women over fifty don't scream, at least not out loud. We smile and wait on our elderly mothers. Jim and I have been primary care givers for my parents for some years. Dad is gone. Mom takes multiple medications for a variety of chronic conditions including heart trouble and a bipolar disorder. We count each day with her as a gift. In the beginning, we put our lives on hold and spoke of the time when things would get back to normal. Gradually, we've come to realize that normal is whatever shows up on our plates each day. It has taken us a long time to arrive at this point of acceptance. Normal for us today is taking care of Mom and our teenage daughter. Normal is never having enough time to pour into the things that interest us the most. We have come to think of life as a wide stream, sometimes bouncing us through perilous rapids and other times letting us drift quietly through back waters. Through it all, faith is the boat that carries us. True, sometimes faith carries us kicking and screaming. Once in a while, we even manage to row a little. Other times, exhausted, we curl up inside our boat and let it carry us where it will.

CLOSING IN ON GOD

Years ago the children and I read a book we really enjoyed about a universe where houses, clothes, and other material things never wore out. In fact, the more use something received, the stronger and more beautiful it became. Lately, it occurs to me that the things that will outlast this world - patience, faith, hope, truth and love do become stronger and more beautiful with use.

Push Button Phones
Jim

A few years ago, our household finally succumbed and bought a push button phone. For years we had held out with our ancient but ever trusty rotary models. They worked perfectly. We felt no need to switch just to be like everybody else. Finally, the day arrived when we decided to purchase an answering machine. To our surprise, we found we had to have a phone that plugged into the wall. For years we had assumed that all phones plugged into the wall. The truth of the matter was that our rotary phones were "hard wired," which, in my way of thinking, meant that we were directly wired to our local phone company and from there to the rest of the world. (You can imagine the trouble I have trying to understand "cellular.")

Now I faced the task of installing a new phone plug. In spite of being reluctant at first, with a lot of coaching from the local phone store and a friend, I became a self-made "phone electrician." Basically, this required an ability to differentiate between black, red, yellow and green wires. When I finished the task and heard that dial tone, I beamed with pride over my new found skill.

CLOSING IN ON GOD

Recently, I used my skill to install a new phone for my mother-in-law. It was my big chance to introduce her to push button technology. After I proudly presented my mother-in-law with her new phone, she never said a word. She just sat and stared for the longest time at the over-sized buttons. I tried to coax her into calling someone, but she put me off till later. I knew by her voice and her look of bewilderment that she intended to go back into the bedroom to use her faithful old rotary when she needed to communicate. Old habits are the hardest to change.

As a young Catholic, I struggled to memorize certain prayers to recite each day at home or in school. It was the way we communicated with God. Over the years, my conversations with God became more spontaneous. Convinced that this was the way to relate to God in my daily life, I left the old prayers behind. Then, a couple of years ago at a retreat, someone placed a rosary on my desk. I gave it a try for old times sake. The familiar words flowed from my lips, and the rosary once more became part of my prayer life. It seems as though the old prayers were the "hard wires" in my faith. They were the direct, approved and comfortable link to our Lord.

Prayers come in many forms. I am grateful for the freedom of expression in our church today, but some things don't lose their value with age. By the way, we do still have one rotary phone in our basement, and it works perfectly.

*****

Patron Saints
Jim

Some forty plus years ago Sister Mary L., a Dominican Sister who was a giant in stature as well as authority, decided that all of us kids at St. Stephen's Elementary would dress up as saints

73

for Halloween. As you can imagine, this didn't go over well with my generation. All of us had other plans. Frankenstein and werewolves were popular back then, but Sister was the principal and the most powerful person in our world. In short, we had no choice. For days, we searched through dusty old books looking for the perfect saint to emulate in colorful garb and, hopefully, be the envy of all the other kids. As it turned out, most of the saints were not known for colorful garb. Many of us showed up in plain old clothes with a saint's name on a sign hung around our necks. The only thing I clearly remember is that there were about ten St. Patricks. The green shamrocks were a dead giveaway.

I did learn something from this exercise. I discovered all kinds of saints designated as patrons for many different groups of people. Farmers, doctors, teachers, mothers, fathers, laborers, even lawyers had someone designated as their patron. I can't recall finding a saint assigned to those of us who are caught up in the second half of life. Who is the patron of the slightly deaf? Which saint watches over those of us with arthritic knees? God knows we need all the help we can get. Is there a saint who had to deal with the demands of adult and semi-adult children while responding to the needs of aging parents, an aging body, an aging home and automobile and a whole host of worn out appliances? If there is, I want that saint on my side.

My mother used to tell me that many saints are known only to God. I believe this is true. As I look around the church I can easily spot many other "second halfers" and I imagine most are praying for patience, guidance and understanding. It is comforting to know we are not alone. Multitudes have gone before us and are at rest with Jesus. Our Savior had many demands placed on Him during his brief ministry on earth. On more than one occasion, He openly expressed His frustration and despair. Yet He never lost sight of his mission. The road in the second half of life can be rocky at times, but it is good to know that we have countless unknown saints who have been exactly where we are, have gone before us and are on our side.

*****

Nellie Poe
Ann

Nellie Poe Powers. Her name had a ring to it, perhaps because she claimed to be a distant relative of a famous Poe, as in Edgar Allan. In the early sixties' the spirit of a youthful president and the "new frontier," inspired our young generation. As idealists at age twenty-two, we headed off with the Peace Corps to Liberia, West Africa, in search of personal answers to some of life's great questions.

Nellie, at sixty-nine, was an "old" idealist, and a fellow volunteer. When we met her, we knew she didn't have to search for anything. We went through training together, a little over a hundred of us kids and Nellie. We exercised, studied, and camped in the Sierras under the stars, and we played. Nellie did it all, keeping up at her own pace.

We knew only a few things about her life. She had retired from teaching in Peoria. Her husband had died and her sons were grown. She was on her own. Her gift of determination, on one hand, made her very endearing. On the other hand, we soon recognized her as someone we might sometimes want to avoid. Nellie always had plans, and if we happened to be nearby, her plans often included us.

Our Peace Corps leadership assigned Nellie to work in Liberia's capital city of Monrovia, where running water and electricity were available. They felt that it would be too rough on her to be stationed in a bush village. However, on most weekends and holidays, Nellie turned up in the remotest of villages. We remember one particular holiday when she insisted we accompany her on an up-country trip in a weatherbeaten taxi. We rode in front while Nellie squeezed her ample frame between two dignified Muslim tribesmen in the back seat. With red dust flying behind us and doors rattling, Nellie ordered everybody to sing. She then broke into a rousing chorus of "Oh Susanna" while she kept pounding on everyone within reach. She forced all of us, including the tribesmen, to sing along in one fashion or another.

By that time, young volunteers were a common sight in the countryside, but an elderly white woman was a curiosity. The villagers dubbed her the "double-old grandmother." She earned the respect and affection of the tribal people because she sat with the women and learned to weave mats or asked them to show her how to cook.

Soon after we returned to the States, we had a letter from Nellie. She asked for information about Samoa because she had decided to go there next. If we learned one all-important lesson from Nellie, it was to keep moving, keep growing. Perhaps to be truly alive, we've got to have plans.

On a larger scale, God himself has plans, not only for His creation as a whole, but for each of us, personally. When we align our plans with God's, we feel a sense of unity and peace. As part of God's plan, we look at life differently. Not only are we alive in Christ now; we anticipate a life to come as part of God's eternity. Nellie had plans that kept her moving forward. Maybe that's why she always seemed young in spite of her years.

Senior Moments
Jim & Ann

One afternoon while we sat on the porch up at Grandma's, a friend walked past. She stopped to talk and soon the conversation turned to mutual acquaintances from years gone by. When she tried to call to mind a certain familiar name, she said, "You know, she was the person who...." No use. Frozen in mid-sentence, she remembered the person, but not the name. Both her hands flew to her face and she exclaimed, "Oh! I'm having a senior moment!" We laughed because this sort of thing often happens to us.

We asked about her husband, Steve, and her children. Soon she resumed her walk. Just before she vanished around the corner, we looked at each other and one of us said, "Her husband's name isn't Steve. It's Ed. Steve is her son." We had experienced our own "senior moment," and our friend had the grace to let it pass.

At this time in our lives, this kind of thing is hardly a rare occurrence. Indeed we sail in dangerous waters, full of deep pools and hidden rocks. At breakfast, we open the microwave oven only to discover that it's still occupied by the vegetable we meant to serve at last night's supper. We sometimes put a telephone number, key, or semi-important paper away in a safe place. When we need to retrieve the item, we have no idea how to locate the safe place. At least, while the younger generation is searching for its identity, we have only to search for lost things.

Experts tell us that short-term memory is one of the first areas to be affected by the aging process. The solution lies in our ability to find ways to compensate. For years, people have kept lists and written notes to themselves. This technique works very well as long as you can remember where you save the notes. In recent years a whole new industry has sprung up with solutions for those of us suffering from "senior moments." Small, hand-held computers can store names, dates, appointments, and those phone numbers that escape us. They can even be programmed to beep as a reminder to keep an appointment. Science has come up with a replacement for Mom and the kitchen calendar.

In spite of our "senior moments," there are some things about which we have no doubts. We know what we believe and who we really are. The people closest to our hearts are certain of our love. We've got the important things covered. As for the rest of life? Never mind the details!

*****

Chairs
Jim

In my youth, furniture was nothing more than a collection of things selected by my parents. The only time it came into focus was when my brothers and I fought for the best spot from which to view the new black and white television. After Ann and I married, furniture became more important as we gradually accumulated a variety of items necessary to the bringing up of children.

For years we sat on our sixties' vintage wood-framed furniture with cushions. No matter how many throw pillows we used, we still ended up with aching backs. Years ago we didn't notice the discomfort so much, or perhaps it just didn't matter. We were so over-committed we never had time to sit very long in one spot. Eventually, we longed for a comfortable place to rest our weary bones.

I can easily bring up childhood memories of my father's overstuffed chair and foot stool. This chair remains the centerpiece of his family room. Here, Dad falls asleep soon after he settles down, much to the delight of all of us. This has long been a source of family humor. When I go home for a visit, I still like to stretch out in his chair for a few minutes of quiet reminiscing.

Probably the oldest chair remaining in our family belonged to Aunt Delia. Occupying a place of honor in the gathering room at my in-laws' home, this chair has an unusual shape with a short back and a long seat. The original upholstery reflects the style of the thirties. In spite of its worn appearance, it is surprisingly comfortable. A gentle rocking motion quickly induces memories of feisty Aunt Delia and the feud she had with a neighbor over a certain pecan tree. We wanted chairs like Dad's or Aunt Delia's to pass on as memory-filled heirlooms.

We celebrated our thirtieth anniversary by gifting ourselves with two special chairs to enjoy for the rest of our lives. After many trial sittings, we decided on a matched set of absolutely wonderful recliners. Most days now, we look forward to getting home and into our chairs. They are a place to refocus our thoughts, to share our ideas and our dreams, and even to pray. We never thought that furniture would make such an impact on our lives. Ann observed that when our chairs are in a reclining position, they resemble the palm of a hand. This brought to mind that beautiful song "On Eagles Wings," with its promise of total peace and comfort in the Lord's hands. In the second half of life, a blessing often comes in the shape of a good chair.

Golden Crumbs
Ann

On the day Mother Teresa died, we happened to be on retreat in the small town of New Harmony, Indiana. We stayed at a beautiful inn known for its quiet simplicity as well as its wonderful food. The weather had turned dry, clear and crisp with the first kiss of autumn. Flowers still bloomed beside the inn doors. A dwarf tree, its limbs heavy with red apples, grew on a trellis against a wall.

It happened that our retreat master, Archabbot Lambert Reilly from St. Meinrad, had also given retreats for Mother Teresa and her Sisters. Throughout the weekend, he shared his memories of times spent with them. Our retreat became a meditation on the power and beauty of a personal life focused completely on Christ. A "golden crumb" had fallen in our laps.

A "golden crumb" is what we've come to call these beautiful, unexpected gifts that fall from the Bread of Life when we least expect them and often when we need them the most. While some people plan for the day when they will win the lottery or save for a trip around the world, we rely on these small unexpected crumbs of joy to provide the seasoning in our stew of life.

The friends who invited us over for a meal and an evening of adult conversation, without knowing what a rare thing this is in our lives, provided a golden crumb we still taste. The son and his wife, who drove five hours to surprise us with a dinner of homemade spaghetti, provided an afternoon of unexpected joy. Golden crumbs are the wilted flowers offered from the hand of a child, the phone call from a friend far away, the rose that blooms in

November, or the mechanic who fixed our car, then insisted that we must take our vacation first and pay him later.

The older we become, the more we realize how priceless it is, not only to catch golden crumbs, but to drop these into the paths of other people. Each golden crumb we catch reminds us that we have the power to spread small gifts before other hungry souls. The deeper we draw our nourishment from the Bread of Life, the easier it becomes to feed other people. We are convinced that if all the lotteries and other pie-in-the-sky schemes designed to make us hungry for things we don't need and can't have were to disappear from the face of the earth, we could still be quite satisfied with nothing more than golden crumbs.

"I will give you a light to the nations."
Isaiah 49:6

Christmas

In the wisdom of our age,
let us be bearers of true light.

Sliding Past Christmas
Jim & Ann

The road gets mighty slippery between Thanksgiving and Christmas. We're not talking about snow and sleet on the highway. We're talking about the Interstate to Physical Destruction. This time of year it's paved with pumpkin pie, cookies, potholes full of gravy and enough melted chocolate to slide right down through the gates of Perdition.

What's worse is, not only are we tempted by an overabundance of delectables; it's our duty to eat Grandma's fruitcake, Aunt Wanda's candy, our neighbor's pies and Cousin Mabel's potluck extravaganzas. The fact that these things all taste heavenly only makes it easier to fulfill our friendly obligations. We repent in the wee hours of the morning while we listen to each other unwrap little packets of Di-Gel in the dark.

Here is the dilemma. With one hand, (the one that does good deeds), we truly recognize that we are the temple of the Spirit. On the other hand, (the one that keeps stuffing in the goodies), we really enjoy celebrating life this season. It's just that every time we turn around, it seems that food is involved in the celebration. Do we set aside our worries for now, only to join the thundering herd repenting of physical weakness after the first of the year? Or do we piously refuse to partake of all cholesterol riches, treating them as unclean? To further complicate our situation, when we take the time to really look at ourselves, it becomes quite obvious that no matter what we give up, our chances of reaching physical perfection are slim to none.

What are we to do? Recently, we bought our daughter a bracelet with WWJD ("What Would Jesus Do?") embossed on it. Not only was it a valuable reminder for her, but it helped us to realize that the guidance we had been searching for was right in front of us, in the Gospels. Jesus often ate in other people's homes. Presumably he enjoyed whatever they served. The thing about supper at Mary and Martha's or anywhere else was that, with one notable exception, our Lord focused on the people involved and not on what He ate. The Last Supper is the only meal we recall where the focus was on food. The fact that Jesus and His friends exercised by walking everywhere certainly didn't hurt either.

That's the way through this season. Focus on the Bread of Life. Enjoy the company of others without paying too much attention to what is being served. And take long walks whenever possible.

*****

Stained Glass Windows
Jim & Ann

During Advent we like to open the treasure chest of our faith and admire some of the beautiful things inside. Among the many things we view with a deep sense of gratitude are stained glass windows. Three thousand years before Christ, Egyptians had learned how to make colored beads of glass. In the days when Christ walked among us, the Romans knew how to blow glass into vessels and make it into transparent sheets. A millennium later, by the 13th century in France, stained glass windows had become the crowning glory of massive cathedrals.

Stained glass came to be known as "painting with light," yet these magnificent works of art had the humblest of beginnings as common grains of sand. It was only when fired to intense degrees that silica from the sand fused into the unity of glass. Four stained glass windows survived a fire at Chârtres Cathedral in 1194. These four windows still exist. Three rise today as part of the west facade of the cathedral.

We think about the ancient craftsmen who went home to their cottages at night with their hands bleeding from their work. We wonder if they ate plain bread while they talked to their sons about what it meant to make stained glass windows. How could they comprehend that their work would survive plagues, wars and famines over the next thousand years?

Simple folk who could not read understood the word of God written in stained glass. Shepherds in fields, angels, Mary and Joseph's flight into Egypt, all lived in the light above them. In the presence of stained glass, peace came, hearts opened and thoughts turned to heaven. Like Joseph's coat of many colors, stained glass sent their heartfelt prayers to heaven wrapped in coats of glory.

Most certainly, the presence of Christ doesn't require stained glass windows. They provide only a quiet symphony of light to the glory of the Eucharist. Somehow, though, it seems we lost something of value when we stopped using stained glass in our worship spaces. We need to preserve this art because through it we remember what Christ does in our lives. Like the Master

Craftsman He is, Christ fits the cut and broken edges of our lives together until His design for us takes shape. When we rise in our places and let His light pass through us, the common sand that we are becomes a magnificent work of art.

*****

Heart Treasures
Jim

During the holiday season, many of us are flooded with memories of other times and places. In our minds, we sometimes travel back to simpler days. The holidays were shorter in that they started at Thanksgiving and ended at New Year's. Instead of shopping malls, we remember stores clustered around major intersections. Often the store owners pooled their resources to put up outside decorations and perhaps a few loudspeakers over which carols played. We greeted neighbors as we walked from store to store, bundled up against freezing Michigan temperatures. We didn't mind the inconvenience because we felt welcome wherever we went. Even strangers seemed friendly.

As a child, I especially remember walking to Midnight Mass. Not only was it the one night we were allowed to stay up so late; the dark stillness gave our whole neighborhood a mystical feeling. . We understood that something most special had come upon us. As we walked to church a block away, our faces numbed in the northern breezes. We hardly noticed. Surrounded by people we loved, our spirits took control and our hearts overflowed with warmth.

Today, things are quite different because some of the people we love the most live far from us. We are reminded in the Gospels that the first Christmas came to Mary and Joseph while they were far from their family and friends. It must have been a difficult time for Mary, giving birth without the wisdom and experience of her older female relatives. One can easily imagine this teen mother trying to nurse her infant for the first time, probably wondering if the baby had enough nourishment. To top it all off, strangers came in with their story of hosts of angels and the marvelous words they heard. After the shepherds arrived and recalled what they had seen, the Gospel of Luke tells us, "Mary treasured all these things and pondered them in her heart."

The holidays we have in the second half of life may be a far cry from our childhood memories. Often we ache to see distant family and friends, forgetting that this is exactly the way the Holy Family spent their first Christmas. In the presence of our Lord, this night became one of Mary's heart treasures. No matter where we are, if Christ is present, we are home. Christmas is a time to relive treasured memories in our hearts.

*****

The Christmas Gift
Ann

On December 21, 1984, in the middle of O'Hare Airport in Chicago, we had a birth in our family. On that morning, we had allowed far more than enough time to drive through the wind, rain and sleet we encountered on the highway with other travelers. Once inside the terminal, Christmas trees twenty feet tall greeted us like sentinels rising from the holiday crowd. Each tree had been carefully decked with bows, packages and teddy bears. People hurried to make connections and everyone appeared to be carrying backpacks, wrapped gifts, skis, or small children.

Even with Christmas in the air, several hours is a long time to wait in a terminal with children. We tried to make the best of it. Young Jim and his sister, Katie, read books they had brought.

Their exhausted Dad, who had been fighting a monster cold for several days, dozed upright on a bench. Our youngest child, Chris, passed the time by watching planes take off and land outside the glass wall of the terminal. We grew tired and hungry while a certain Northwest Orient jet from Korea was delayed, and then delayed again.

One by one, the hours trickled by until nightfall when the call came to gather at the arrival gate. We groaned a few minutes later when yet another delay dashed our hopes. Nearby, one desperate mom tried to pacify her cranky kids by pumping quarters into a pay television. When the quarters ran out and the cartoons stopped, the kids fought with each other, thus providing a free diversion for everyone else.

Another mother had costumed her three children as Christmas gifts in large, decorated cardboard boxes with their arms and legs sticking out. She had a "Welcome Home Daddy" tag attached to each of them. They ran around bumping into each other as well as into bystanders. I leaned close to Chris and whispered, "Aren't you glad we didn't make you dress up like that?" A sweet smile of gratitude crossed his face.

Sometime after dark, the long-awaited jet taxied within a few feet of the glass wall where we waited. Soon, the human Christmas presents welcomed their Daddy. Grandparents hugged the grumpy grandchildren and the crowd thinned. Finally, a slight man climbed off with a round-faced, screaming, dark-haired pink bundle. I held out my arms, and in the middle of one of the busiest airports in the world, on the busiest weekend of the year, an elderly Korean social worker handed me our youngest child. She sagged her head against my shoulder and grew still and quiet, just as though she knew she had come home.

I couldn't see her face because she had slumped against me with her head turned away. So, instead, I watched the faces of Jim and the children. Touching her hair, holding her fingers, they made a tight circle around us. "She's beautiful. She's so beautiful," they whispered. Time slowed as we stood together in a widening pool of light. Nearby, an elderly woman tugged on her husband's sleeve and they stopped at the edge of our circle. A young man with a pink Mohawk haircut, earrings and black leather vest smiled shyly and then paused. The light crossed the face of a weary man in a faded green trench coat. The circle grew while Christmas flooded one crowded corner of the world, touched us all, and changed our lives forever.

*****

Peace in Christ

Jim Cavera holds a Masters Degree in Social Work from Michigan State University. For the past 30 years, he has worked as a psychiatric and medical social worker. Currently, Jim is the social worker for the Senior Health Program at St. Mary's Medical Center in Evansville, Indiana. He also serves as a deacon to St. Mary Church, Evansville.

Ann Cavera holds a Masters Degree in Education. For many years she taught school at the middle school level. Until March of 1999, she worked as an Admissions Counselor in a community college. In addition, Ann served as the primary care giver for her elderly parents for five years. Currently, she is the Director of Religious Education at St. Mary Church.

Jim and Ann are the parents of four children, ages 18-33. They are both experienced speakers and often create and present workshops on a wide range of topics. For the past four years they have co-authored **The Second Half**, a column for Catholics over the age of fifty. Nationwide, **The Second Half** appears in nine publications with a combined circulation of approximately 300,000. Jim and Ann received the Catholic Press Association's First Place Award for a general commentary newspaper column in 1999. "The Second Half" also received a second place award in 2001.

CLOSING IN ON GOD

Additional copies of *Closing In On God*
may be ordered from:

Cavera/Midlife Spirit
1280 Cross Gate Dr.
Evansville, IN 47710

Name _____

Address _____

_____

City _____ State _____ Zip _____

E-Mail Address (optional) _____

_____ Copies at $8.00 per copy $ _____

Indiana residents add $0.40 tax per copy $ _____

Shipping and handling $2.00 per copy $ _____

Total $ _____